D0833449

ONCE THEY HEAR MY NAME

"This is a book for everyone who's adopted a child, from Korea or anywhere. The honest voice of each adoptee makes for riveting reading and provides a window into the lives, minds and hearts of these children -- almost all of whom wrestle with not just occasional teasing, but more profoundly, with the best way to cope with two histories: two families -- one birth and one adoptive -- the duality that's at the core of their being."

— Judy Woodruff, TV Journalist and adoptive mother

"Ever wonder what those adorable Asian children think about their transracial, adoptive American lives? In this important, groundbreaking book, the long overdue voices of Korean American adoptees, grown-up and reflective, tell their stories with rare insight and breathtaking emotional honesty."

— Helen Zia, author *Asian American Dreams: The Emergence of an American People*

ONCE THEY HEAR MY NAME

*Korean adoptees and their
journeys toward identity*

Ellen Lee   Marilyn Lammert   Mary Anne Hess

Tamarisk Books
Silver Spring, Maryland

COPYRIGHT © 2008 by Ellen Lee, Marilyn Lammert and Mary Anne Hess

ALL RIGHTS RESERVED UNDER INTERNATIONAL AND PAN-AMERICAN COPYRIGHT CONVENTIONS.
PUBLISHED IN THE UNITED STATES BY TAMARISK BOOKS, SILVER SPRING, MARYLAND

This book, or parts, thereof, may not be reproduced in any form without permission.

Tamarisk Books
P.O. Box 3006
Silver Spring, MD 20918
www.tamariskbooks.com

LIBRARY OF CONGRESS CONTROL NUMBER: 2007937159

ISBN: 978-0-9793756-0-6 (13 digit soft cover)
ISBN: 0-9793756-0-6 (10 digit soft cover)
ISBN: 978-0-9793756-1-3 (13 digit hard cover)
ISBN: 0-9793756-1-4 (10 digit hard cover)

Book & Cover Design by
Nancy Vala Michaels

MANUFACTURED IN THE UNITED STATES OF AMERICA
SIGNATURE BOOK PRINTING, www.sbpbooks.com

*To all the adoptees.
Their willingness to tell their stories
turned the idea of this book into a reality.*

INTRODUCTION

At some point in our growing up, usually during adolescence, the question of who we are looms large and the quest for answers is intense. For Korean adoptees, the quest is first and foremost the struggle for racial identity. Because they are born of one race and culture, but most often raised in another, this task can be much more intricate and extended. Adoptees have varying degrees of access to the support of family or friends with similar experiences. Their white parents have not experienced the racial discrimination, name calling and teasing that many adoptees often face. Sometimes they may be the only Koreans or persons of color in their schools or communities. The stories in this book trace the complex issues confronted by nine adoptees and their creative, individual paths toward resolution.

The oldest Korean adoptees now living in the United States are those adopted by American GIs stationed in Korea during the war and its aftermath in the early to mid-1950s. Ravaged by long years of conflict, Korea was a place where thousands of orphaned, homeless children roamed the streets. Immediately after the war, Pearl S. Buck, the American author and human rights activist, brought many Korean orphans and Amerasians, fathered by American soldiers, to the United States for adoption through her agency, Welcome House. In 1955 an Oregon farmer named Harry Holt traveled to Korea and brought back eight orphans whom he and his wife Bertha adopted. The following year the couple established an adoption program in Korea. The adoptions that began as a humanitarian effort to rescue orphaned, mostly

Amerasian, children continued for many reasons, including: ongoing poverty in certain segments of the Korean population, the stigma surrounding illegitimacy, and the lack of cultural precedents for Koreans to adopt outside their family bloodlines.

Harry and Bertha Holt's efforts eventually grew into Holt International, which has placed more than 60,000 children from Korea with U.S. families over the past 50 years. Various estimates put the total number of Korean adoptees in the U.S. between 100,000 and 120,000. Although the number of visas granted each year to Korean orphans has slowed (from a peak of about 6,000 in the mid-1980s to 1,630 in 2005), the U.S. Census Bureau reports that Korea still ranks as the largest single-country source of foreign-born adoptees under age 18 -- with about 48,000 children currently fitting into this category. In recent years Korea has experienced a mixture of criticism and embarrassment over the large number of its children adopted abroad. Government efforts are underway to reduce this number by encouraging domestic adoption.

In the years since the first Korean orphans arrived in the United States, American society has come to accept family building through adoption across all kinds of racial, ethnic and national divides. Some of this acceptance came about out of necessity. With the widespread use of birth control and the fading of traditional taboos surrounding unwed mothers, the number of babies available for adoption domestically dwindled. In addition, the increased acceptance of interracial relationships and their multiracial offspring has also opened the way, in many communities, for families with members of many hues. Also, millions of immigrants from Latin America, Africa and Asia have become part of the fabric of our small towns, as well as our large urban areas. It's not unusual to find places in the U.S. with such a mixture of races and cultures that there has ceased to be a "majority" group.

Recent census figures show that 4 percent (1.7 million) of U.S. family households include adopted children. About 13 percent of the adoptees are foreign-born and about 17 percent are of a different race than at least one of their adoptive parents. China, Russia and Guatemala are now the top three countries of birth for new adoptees coming to the U.S. As these children grow, they and their parents can look to the long-time experiences of Korean adoptees for guidance in coming to grips with the difficult questions of identity formation in families that transcend racial and ethnic categorization.

By the early 1990s a critical mass of Korean adoptees was reaching adulthood, and seeking cultural roots. Some started traveling to their homeland alone or in groups. Many formed support groups in large cities such as Los Angeles, New York and Minneapolis to seek out each other in settings where their experiences as Korean adoptees in white America could be shared and understood. Since 1999, KAAN (Korean American Adoptee Adoptive Family Network) has held yearly conferences bringing together adoptees and their families from throughout the U.S. and Canada.

Co-editors Ellen Lee and Marilyn Lammert met in May 1994 as Marilyn was planning a trip with her 11-year-old son Adam to Korea, his birthplace. A mutual friend had suggested they talk. Ellen, who was born in Korea, emigrated to the United States at age 10 with her family and, like Marilyn, had spent her professional life as a social worker/therapist.

Ellen's initial response was: "What do I have to say about

Korea? I've lived here for so long." But she soon discovered she did have something to say and was very helpful, easing Marilyn's anxiety and offering lots of information. They met again after Marilyn and Adam returned from Korea and continued getting together, going to adoption conferences, reading and talking about adoption in a small group of other social workers.

With Adam's encouragement Marilyn continued searching for his birth family and, in 1996, learned that their contacts in Korea had located them. Adam's wish was that Marilyn meet them first, which meshed with Ellen's suggestion that she and Marilyn travel to Korea together. This time they had names of several adult Korean adoptees living in Korea to meet and, as they talked to them, they gathered more names of adoptees living there, often for work or study. Along the way they had chance meetings with adoptees who had come to Seoul to search for their birth families. The common theme emerging from these encounters was the quest for self-definition and, as part of that pursuit, the adoptees' need to know their Korean roots. As Ellen and Marilyn listened, they were struck by the different paths each adoptee had taken to reach that point.

The two came up with the idea of collecting adoptees' stories. It was clear that identity was a major issue, as well as a complex and evolving one, so they decided to pull together these stories by asking questions that focused on identity development. They wanted to let adoptees tell in their own words what it was like to grow up with parents of a different race and to let them tell in detail the stories of their struggles and their triumphs. They also wanted to remain sensitive to the fact that the adoptees were dealing with decisions made for them by others, and that they needed to tell their stories in their own ways, unhampered by outside analysis or judgment.

Adoptees are experts on their own lives, on their own identities, on how they became the adults they are today. Different people create different story lines and our collection shows with certainty that there is no one formula for developing identity.

For one adoptee, taking on the German-Catholic identity of her parents seemed natural until fifth grade when taunts of "Chinaman" propelled her to beat up the tormenter. Even so, her quest to connect with her heritage didn't begin in earnest until age 38 after she experienced trouble on the job because her manager had lost relatives in the Korean War. Another remembers that, as a youngster, all he wanted was not to look different from his white parents and blond, curly-haired brother. Being Asian, he says, seemed to peg him as a "perpetual foreigner." As a teenager, he gradually started identifying more with his black classmates who also faced race-based stereotypes and discrimination.

Two adoptees in this book have searched successfully for their birth families in Korea and traveled thousands of miles for emotional and, as one describes, "surreal" reunions connecting them to birthparents, brothers and sisters. Others have looked to no avail, but still say they felt a real sense of "coming home" when they touched down in their country of birth. As one adoptee explains, "I looked like everyone else. It was the first time that I felt like I belonged. No one looked at me like I was a foreigner."

In their stories the adoptees tell how, over the years, they've continued to try to reconcile their American upbringing with their Korean roots. Perhaps the greatest challenge for adoptive parents, who've grown up in biological families, is that they can't rely on their own life experiences to help their children grapple with this basic issue. And, there are no foolproof guidelines for how to help a child deal with transracial adoption. "It all depends on the kid," says one adoptee who resisted her mother's initial attempts to expose her to Korean culture. "As I started to reach adolescence I was aware of being different and then I would try to ignore it or deny it for awhile."

One mother described in the book relied on the advice of social workers who told her to "Americanize" her newly adopted 3-year-old daughter because it would "confuse" her to find out anything about Korean culture. As a result the adoptee says, "I always thought of myself as white. It was when I looked into the mirror or saw the looks on people's faces when I was with my family that I remembered I wasn't."

For other parents the Americanization wasn't as deliberate. "Growing up in a rural area, I really didn't have any contact with Koreans or other Asians," remembers one adoptee. "My parents never tried to bring Korean influences into my upbringing. We had Chinese food, maybe once a year, never had a bowl of rice. I don't know if they purposely did that or not, but their intentions were always to make me feel like the rest of the kids."

Other adoptees talk about parents who made concerted efforts to expose their children to their heritage. For one adoptee, a week at Korean culture camp as a young teen marked the first time she felt okay talking about adoption. "It was good to have people who understood or felt similar feelings about being adopted and not always wanting to be Asian, maybe wanting to be white or Caucasian, or whatever you want to call it, for a little while," she says. "We talked about maybe wanting to find our birthparents, what kind of discrimination we faced, and then, with my peers, we all came up with ways to deal with it. It was a really nice support system . . . we got to eat Korean food, learn some Korean songs and prayers . . . I was very inspired to learn more about the country that gave me birth."

The stories in this book illustrate the wide variety of ways adoptive parents and adoptees have wrestled with the issues surrounding identity formation. The subject is far too complex for a one-size-fits-all approach. However, this we do know: Being adopted is bound to alter a child's life experiences in very fundamental ways. Coming to that understanding isn't easy for parents, but perhaps these stories can help by telling all of us something about the very human process of developing identity.

❖

A brief explanation of how we wrote the book ...

Several years ago we took out an advertisement in *Korean Quarterly* seeking adoptees to participate in our project. A number of adoptees responded with some submitting pieces they had written of their own recollections growing up. We also developed a list of possible interviewees through personal contacts and our work in the adoption field. Those who made the final cut for the book represent -- as much as possible -- a diversity of gender, age, geography, experiences and viewpoint.

Using an audiotape recorder, Ellen Lee interviewed all the adoptees, either in person or by phone. She used a general list of questions we had developed, which were designed to elicit factual information as well as to delve into our central question of identity formation. However, each interview inevitably took off in its own direction, reflecting the individuality of each adoptee. Marilyn Lammert participated in some of the interviews and transcribed all the tapes. Because we interviewed each adoptee at least twice, we realized that organizing the book in a simple question-and-answer format would not work. In each case Mary Anne Hess edited the multiple interviews into a single first-person narrative. To make sure the stories reflect their authentic voices, all the adoptees have read and approved the final versions, making changes when needed.

The identifying information for adoptees at the end of the chapters reflects their ages, professions and places of residence close to the time of publication, not at the time of their interviews.

About our title...

Most Korean adoptees grapple with the mismatch between their faces and their last names. Whether this divergence results in a few curious looks, momentary confusion or invasive queries, it certainly can be the catalyst for bringing issues of identity and adoption to the forefront.

When interviewing the adoptees we heard a number of anecdotes with this mismatch as their common thread. The words that inspired our title are those of Todd Knowlton who talks about his experiences in Chapter Four:

"When I got to college I said I was adopted right off the bat. I would always bring it up – even today – because, I mean, there's no hiding. It doesn't bother me but *once they hear my last name*, people always ask uncomfortable questions."

❖

And, finally ...

We have come to accept adoption as a continuing process. For some adoptees, more than others, identity resolution becomes a life-long struggle. It is this hard-fought process, this struggle -- whether conscious or unconscious -- that we hope you can hear in the thoughtful voices of the adoptees who speak out on these pages.

Marilyn Lammert
Ellen Lee
Mary Anne Hess
Fall 2007

TABLE OF CONTENTS

Photo gallery in center of book

Adam

Around age 7 or so I started asking my parents why I looked different from most of my friends. I had the feeling they had been waiting for me to ask, so they sat me down and they explained to me, the best they could, about adoption.

I think they had always told my sister Katie and me that we were adopted, always leaving books around the house about adoption or about different ways that families are created. I flipped through them when I was little, but I didn't really understand them, I don't think. Then it gradually kind of began to sink in.

I don't think there was a specific instance that prompted me to ask why I looked different. I think I just looked in the mirror one day and realized I had much darker hair, a slightly darker

1

complexion and different eye shape from the majority of my friends. So, I guess I just went up to my parents one day and said, "Mom, Dad, why do I look different?"

Part of it, I think, was also finally realizing that, hey, wait a second, my whole family looks a lot different than I do. Even my sister is Caucasian -- she's Pennsylvanian, and so she could more easily pass as a natural child of my parents. My mom tells me stories of how, when she was walking around with my sister and me, people would look at us strangely, point at me and ask, "Is he yours?"

I don't remember anything specifically like that. Much later, in high school, I remember walking around with my sister, who's only seven months older, and people asking us if we were going out. We would just look at each other and say, "Oooo, no."

I don't recall my parents' exact explanation for why I looked different, and I don't remember feeling bad or feeling angry. I just remember thinking, oh well, that kind of explains it. My mom's a social worker who specializes in dealing with adoption, and so she and my dad answered my questions as best as they could, being as upfront as they could, and explaining in ways that hopefully I would understand.

Around the time I was 9, my parents tell me, I started asking questions about my birth family, asking why they gave me up for adoption, where they are now, things like that. I guess it was just something that occurred to me at that point. And then my sister started asking questions about her birthparents, kind of prompted by me, I guess. My parents never shied away from the questions. If they could answer them they would, and if they couldn't, they'd say, "Well, we don't know, but we can try to find out." They always had an

2

answer that seemed good enough. And, I don't think I was overly adamant about trying to find my birth family or information about them.

By that time I definitely already knew about Korea. In addition to books about adoption, we had books about Korean culture lying around, all over the place, and I would read them. These were little information books about Korea, saying Korea is located here, it has a population of this, it's roughly the size of Indiana, here are some different things that people eat in Korea, different customs, what holidays they celebrate, or how to say a few things in Korean.

I knew little bits and pieces about the culture, how to play the game with the four sticks, the ones that are flat on one side and rounded. I forget what it's called, but we had that and I liked to play that a lot.

I don't remember anything in particular triggering the questions about my birth family, but I just know I started asking and I don't think I ever really let it go. I think from then on it was always in the back of my mind, and every now and then I would think to myself, gee, I wonder what my birth family is like, and I wonder how life would be different if I was still with them. But, since I really didn't know anything about them, I couldn't answer any of my questions.

I wanted to know more, just general information, and I think it's every adoptee's fantasy to be able to meet their birth family. Some people may not necessarily want to meet them, but they always wonder who they were and where they came from, I think. That's something that I've picked up on with a lot of adoptees I've met and talked to.

Around this same time, I really started experiencing teasing for the first time. I got glasses. I went to a different school in fourth grade, to a two-year program for gifted and

3

talented students. I got plopped down in a different environment, with different people. I had always been kind of small for my age compared with most of my friends, but for some reason, I think everything was a little magnified there.

The teasing was mostly based on my race or my ethnicity. People calling me "Chinese eyes," or doing the thing where they pull their eyes thin, asking me if I knew karate, saying mock Chinese words to me, or words that they thought sounded like Chinese. It wasn't constant, only a few isolated incidents, but I was pissed off. I didn't like it one bit. And, it hurt me, but I didn't know exactly why at the time. I just knew that I didn't like it.

I told my parents about it. And I forget exactly what we did. We may have told the school counselor. I think I really had a bad time at that school, and I think I've tried to block most of it out of my memory.

I guess this added to my sense of being different. Also, my parents told me that they had noticed that I was being kind of obliquely teased by my peers at my old elementary school. I personally don't remember, but that's what they say. So, I could have felt left out, or not really ostracized, but kind of liked to a lesser degree, I guess. I don't remember, or I've blocked it out.

In middle school, I experienced much more teasing. Everyone was beginning to go through adolescence, and everyone was awkward, very self-conscious, and then there was me. I had glasses and I was shorter than everyone else. I went through puberty early, so my voice started breaking in sixth grade and I started getting acne. Cliques started forming. People made new friends and broke off old friendships, and it was just a very, very awkward, un-fun time. I like to say that I think that middle school should be stricken

4

from the collective record, just because I've met very, very few people who had a positive middle-school experience.

For example, there was this one kid I had been friends with in my neighborhood elementary school, and then in seventh grade, in the middle of the year, he started calling me "chink" for no apparent reason. That just kind of came out of the blue and that was, I think, the first time I really started getting hurt emotionally by racism, or by name-calling. The other times it had been people I didn't know, weren't my age, or I didn't hang out with. But this was one of my best friends, and that really, really hurt.

I just tried to ignore it, which is what I had been told was the best way to cope. But, I mean, I could ignore it on the surface, but I couldn't really ignore it internally, so I stopped hanging out with him. It never came up again. I think he may have called me names a few more times that year, but that was pretty much it. He was much nicer in high school. I guess he grew up, but, regardless, I still remember that as my first real kick in the face because it just came out of the blue and was from someone I considered to be a good friend. He was someone I'd talked to about being adopted, or at least knew I was adopted and knew I was Korean.

I think he was just doing it to be malicious, maybe he wasn't very sure of himself, and he wanted to make himself feel better by putting someone else down, and that someone happened to be me. I guess I've always kind of felt that I was kind of an easy target for other people -- I was smaller than everyone else, racially different, and I wore glasses. I'd been to that gifted school, so there was that kind of smart air about me, and I got good grades in middle school . . . well, most of middle school.

I'm not sure if adoption ever really played that big a role

5

in the teasing in middle school. It was just the fact that I was Korean. The most immediate thing that set me apart was my skin color because the schools that I went to never really had a very high Asian population. However, adoption did play a big role in how I saw myself. That was how I defined myself, as the Korean, and as the adoptee.

The summer between sixth and seventh grade, my mom and I visited Korea for about a week and a half, just before I turned 12. We went sightseeing in Seoul and Kyongju and traveled to Daegu because that's where I was born. We were trying, I guess, to get a sense of where I came from. In addition to sightseeing, we also wanted to visit the adoption agency, Eastern Child Welfare Society, where we hoped to get more information about my birth family. That's the one my birthmother had worked with, that had placed me in a foster home and then in my adoptive home. We met my foster mother who had by that time retired. She had fostered over 40 babies in her career. We met her actually a couple of times and talked to her through translators. We visited the clinic where I was born in Daegu. My mom and our translator, who was a university student in Seoul, went to look at the house that my birth family had lived in at the time I was born. They offered to take me to see it, but I didn't want to go because earlier that day, we had received some information including my birthmother's name and her age and my birthfather's age. And we found out I had three older brothers and we got the street address and the information about my birth in the clinic where I was delivered. I think it was just too much for me, too much information.

It was all new information. It all just came out of nowhere, almost. People had told us there was no information, and then we haggled with a social worker a little while,

6

and she came out with that. It's a lot for a 12-year-old to take in, and that night my mom and I had a huge argument in the hotel.

The argument with my mom wasn't about anything in particular. It was just everything I had internalized during that day came out against my mom. I think just because all the information kind of overwhelmed me, and I didn't know what to think, and it made me confused and angry. It just put me in a mood not to deal with anyone else and I think that's one of the reasons I didn't want to go see the house, just because it would have been too much. I really didn't know how to put my feelings into words at that time, and I'm still not sure if I do.

Over the years, that's kind of been the way I deal with anger and frustration. I bottle it up and then, if someone offers themselves as a whipping boy, whether they want to or not, I unleash my fury on them. It's funny but for whatever reason, more often than not, it's my mom, just because she knows how to push my buttons whether she likes to or not.

Even though I didn't go to see where my birthparents had once lived, I did look at the pictures my mom took. We have them somewhere. I don't know . . . I just kind of leafed through them. I tried not to pay too much attention when I looked at them.

It was my idea in the first place to go to Korea, not necessarily to search for information, but just to get an idea of where I was coming from and what my homeland was like. Really, except for that one little incident, I enjoyed it. I had a really good time and I think for the most part, my mom did too. It's just an amazing country. We visited a folk village and various temples, and all the big museums -- just really, really amazing stuff.

7

The trip kind of gave me more of an idea of who I was because prior to that I really had never met too many Koreans. I had seen a lot of Koreans at the culture camps I went to here, but there I guess I was just inundated. Just being in Seoul, looking down the street, and just seeing waves and waves of people with black hair, I thought for once nobody could identify me by saying, "Oh yeah, he's the Korean one with glasses." For the first time it was my mom, not me, who stood out in a crowd. I think it was definitely a positive experience for me. At least that's how I remember it.

I think it was important because it gave me more of a sense of the culture that I had come out of and more of an understanding of why I was adopted. At that point I was beginning to read about Confucianism and beginning to understand more of the Confucian way of thinking and about its rigid societal structure. I found out that my family was very poor and they had already had three children, and so from there we figured out that I had been given up because they wouldn't have been able to support me.

Prior to that we had known pretty much close to nothing, not even had my birthmother's name. We knew my family name, which was Woo, and then a proper name, Sang Jin, that my social worker had given me.

The information we got on the trip was much more than we had before, much more than we imagined we would get. We hadn't expected to discover much and then suddenly we find out the street address, that I had siblings, that I had come from an actual family. That information alone was a startling amount, and in a sense, it was overwhelming.

I was pretty young when I made that first visit, but I think it really actually helped me. It told me that I came from an actual family, which may have in some way increased my hopes, or increased my chances of finding my birth family. I had imagined that if my birthmother was very young and not married when I was born, but was married now, she wouldn't want me to find her for fear her husband might find out. Discovering I had been born into an actual family meant there was a chance they would still be together and might be more willing to meet me if I found them.

A couple years later, at the end of eighth grade or so, a friend of ours found our birth family. It had been about four years since we started searching and it kind of came out of the blue. Our friend had a friend in Korea who was a doctor, 70 years old, and a former professor at a medical school in Daegu. He was fairly high up on the Confucian scale of respect, and I think basically he just went into the dong office (the place where all citizen registration information is kept) in Daegu and sat there until they gave him what he wanted. We found out the names, ages and occupations of all the members of my birth family, their address, what other family I had, that my oldest brother was married and had two kids.

That was all pretty overwhelming and I forget exactly how I reacted to that, but I don't think it was anything bad. And then we made arrangements quickly, and my mom visited Korea in May 1996 and met with my birth family. We spent a lot of time before that trying to figure out what she would say to them, finding pictures of me for them to keep, and preparing a letter from me to give to them. We decided it would be best for my mom to visit first, to kind of act as a go-between or an icebreaker between my birth family and me, to see if they would want to meet me in the future. We all decided that was the best course of action, because then, hopefully, my meeting them wouldn't be quite as awkward.

9

I felt it would be very awkward to meet them under any circumstances, but having my mom meet them first would make it less so. We exchanged letters with the youngest of my older brothers a couple of times, I think, and he sent us some photocopied photographs of the family and even though they were very fuzzy, we were able to make out a few things. Then my mom went to Korea, met with them, and videotaped the meeting so I could watch it when she came back.

I was almost 14. I don't remember exactly how I reacted to the tape, but I think I pretty much basically detached my mind from my body. That's the best way I can sum up how I approached it.

The most immediate thing I saw were people who looked like me. It was really the first time that had happened. I'd always kind of wondered what they looked like and where I had gotten some of my traits from, my body shape, my stature, little things like that. I saw that they are all about my size and had a very similar build to me. If I spoke Korean, my voice would have sounded like theirs. And, it was . . . quite something.

I know it's very different from a lot of search stories, to have an adoptive mother meet the birthparents first, before the adoptee. I think it worked out for the best because when my mom met with my birthmother and father and one of my brothers, my birthmother told my mom that she really wanted to meet me. I think my birthmother said not a day went by that she didn't think about me.

I don't remember exactly how it made me feel at the time, but I think it made me feel a lot better about the situation, a lot more eager to meet them in the future. I finally knew that it had been a very tough choice for her, that she sincerely wanted to meet me, and that she cared about me. If I forget everything else in this life, that's the one thing I'll hold onto.

It's just a very powerful thing to say about the one son you had that you had to part with. She already had three sons, but she explained to my mom that she just felt unable to give me the opportunities that she wanted to, that the best life she could provide me with would be one apart from her. I could just tell when she was speaking that it had been a tremendous decision for her and that she had thought about it, given it as much thought as she could.

In a sense I'm still a little bitter because I ended up not growing up with my birthmother, but I know she was thinking about my best interests the whole time. Later, after I actually met my birth family, my adoptive mother felt, for a little while, that maybe she wanted to know if I still thought of her as my mother. She wanted to know if my feelings about her had changed after I'd met the woman who had carried me for nine months and delivered me.

I told her that she was still my mother because she raised me. She was the one who cared for me when I was an infant, and the one who brought me up and taught me all my life lessons and that's what makes her a mother. Even if she didn't physically give birth to me, she's the one who's had the biggest influence on me, and so she will never fail to be my mother in my eyes. There was never a time when I questioned that.

Of course, there were times when I was angry about being adopted. I don't remember if I ever told my parents that I wish I were still in Korea. If anybody asked them, they might say otherwise, but I don't remember that happening. I think at times I was angry with my birthmother for giving

11

me up, but I always thought, always in the back of my mind, that she wanted to give me a better life. And when I found out that was the truth, I think that negated the anger, any anger that I felt about the situation.

After my mom met my birth family, it gave me a better sense of myself because I was able to fully flesh out more of my feelings about them. Being able to actually see them on tape really helped, I think, and being able to understand more of their background and my birthmother's reason for giving me up. It answered some of my questions and put me more at ease with being adopted. Those are the big parts.

I was able to fill in a few blank spaces. When you don't have answers I think you feel more confused about your adoption, about your background, and then about your life. If you can't answer one question, then you can't answer more questions following that one. Being able to say, okay, I know my birthmother gave me up because she had to and she gave me up to give me a better chance in life allows me to say, okay, well, then I was loved from the beginning, and okay, my mother has been thinking about me these past 14 years, and okay, she was concerned about me from the beginning, and she wanted what was best for me. Then that makes me think, okay, so then I am loved.

Before I found all this out, I don't remember feeling that I hadn't been loved. In retrospect that feeling may have been present, especially when I was thinking, why was I given up for adoption? Was it because I was a product of an illicit relationship? Is it because my birthparents were too young to take care of me, or was it because they couldn't take care of me because of their economic status? How did my birthmother feel about me? Was she angry with me for being born? Was she eager to give me up? Was she sad to give me up?

My whole family, my parents and my sister and I, went to Korea to meet my birth family in April 1998. We were there for about a week and it was more business than pleasure, I guess you could say. My dad had always wanted to visit, because of books he had read about Korea or by Korean authors, and from having a Korean child. His father had served as a colonel in the Korean War so my dad had always been interested in the culture and in the country. I think he probably would have wanted to have spent more time sightseeing, but . . . I hate to sound egotistical . . . I was the focus of that visit.

The main goal of that trip was to get me to meet my birth family, which we had arranged in advance. We had waited for a couple of years, after my mom had met them, and my parents said to me that we would go whenever I felt I was ready. At that point I think I was. I think I was as ready as I could be.

I met them on Easter Sunday in a restaurant in Daegu, and I just remember feeling nervous, nervous, nervous. Just before we went into the room in the back of the restaurant where we were to meet, I felt like I was going to faint. I just felt this wave of nausea come over me, and I think my sister noticed. She had met her birthmother a couple of years before so she kind of knew what I was going through, and we talked about that a lot on the trip.

It was interesting because when the door opened, I remember sunlight streaming through the window in the back of the room and just being able to see the dim silhouette of my birthmother, who was the first person I saw and recognized. And for the whole lunch, I just remember kind of being there but not really, kind of like I was floating. It was more like I was taking in the situation and reacting to it instead of actually experiencing it. The first thing my birth-mother said to me was what she had told my mom, that not a day went by that she hadn't thought about me, and she hoped that I wasn't angry that she gave me up. And I told her that I wasn't, that I wasn't angry at her in any way because she had been thinking about what would be best for me when she made her decision.

It was very, very surreal, I would have to say, and I don't regret it at all. I think it was very positive, something that I had been wanting to do for years and I'm pretty sure I was mature enough at that age, or I was comfortable enough with myself to meet them. I'm just replaying it in my mind, just remembering everything, little bits and pieces of the meeting, and remembering what they looked like, what they were wearing, little things that they said. My birthfather told me to respect my parents and love my sister, and do well in school, very Confucian things to say. It's all very hazy, almost dreamlike. And I think for a long time that affected me.

About seven or eight months after the trip, I started experiencing depression, and I think some of that may have stemmed from meeting my birth family. I started seeing a therapist and he thought that my birth family played a bigger part in my life, in my mental life, than I realized. To an extent I think he's right, that they are always nestled somewhere in the back of my mind. I don't think about my birth family on a regular basis . . . I don't think about them that often, but I think, on some level, they are always present. I just know that a few months after I met them, I started feeling really sad. I don't know if meeting my birth family triggered depression, or if it had actively anything to do with it. I just know that all of a sudden I wasn't all that happy.

I've been thinking about that for the last few years and

14

I'm still not sure. Maybe it makes sense because my secret hopes and dreams had always been to meet my birth family. What was I left with after I did that? It's as if to say, I've met them, now what? And, I don't think . . . I don't think I was able to answer that. Putting an end to such a large part of my life left me kind of empty.

I don't really have any kind of continuing relationship with my birth family. We've written to my oldest brother a couple of times, but that's about all. If they're anything like me, then they take some prodding to write or write back. I'm not sure I have any hopes or fantasies about building a relationship with them. I certainly don't have anything in the back of my mind as big as wanting to meet them in the first place.

I've given a lot of thought to what adoption has done to me mentally, and I think that because of adoption, I'm more sensitive to rejection, to feeling distanced from somebody, or more sensitive to loss in general. Like a fear I've always had is that I'll be taken somewhere and abandoned, or I'll be forgotten about. For example, junior year in high school I did a lot of theater, and after a show I was waiting for my sister to pick me up. Then we were supposed to go see a family therapist. As it turns out that was cancelled, but I didn't know, and I sat waiting for her for over an hour. I remember thinking to myself, gee, what if they've just forgotten about me and gone to the appointment without me because I tried calling and no one answered.

I remember reading the developmental theories of Erik Erikson, the psychoanalyst who said that the first experiences really shape a child's mindset. Particularly positive experiences will make you optimistic through life, and negative experiences will make you pessimistic. If anything, I'm

15

certainly pessimistic to a point and I think that may stem, if Erikson is right, from being separated from my birthmother at such an early age, at pretty much one day. Also, maybe because I was distanced from my birth family, I think I'm able to easily distance myself from many things, such as my feelings. I don't know how much of that would translate to other adoptees, but that's what I feel. I think that's the basic impact adoption has had on me, how it has shaped my mindset. I'd call those aspects the negatives, and the positives, I guess, would be that being adopted makes me strive for independence more. Sometimes that can also be a bad thing. For example, if I try to deal with all my problems myself, then things just end up getting worse after a while.

I think the sad feelings I had after meeting with my birth family have abated. I don't think adoption, or meeting my birth family had everything to do with the depression that I went through. I think I'm certainly in a much better mental state now than I was a few years ago and I think that's happened through more internal revelations and through working through a lot of things with a therapist. I guess every now and then, it pokes its head up again, but for the most part I think I've dealt with it.

I've been able to build up really good friendships with several people, but I haven't, for whatever reason, done much dating. And I don't know why that is, to tell you the truth. I don't think it has anything to do with being adopted. It might have more to do with my height because, on average, I'm still about six inches shorter than the majority of my friends. Maybe it was just that in high school girls weren't as interested in dating me because they're just not as sure of themselves to be dating someone shorter than they are, or who looks different from most people. But I really

16

don't know . . . that's their deal.

If there was anything I could have changed about the environment I grew up in, I would like to have seen more Asian faces. As it was, in school I started on a path that I called "destroying Asian stereotypes one by one." I have no aptitude for math or chemistry. I almost failed high school physics, and I don't know how to program anything besides a VCR or car radio stations. I suppose my existence as one of a handful of Asians made me stand out a little in school, and I decided I didn't want to be pigeonholed into any of the convenient pre-conceived types. Of course, my name confused people too. At the beginning of my senior year in high school, all the students in my math class were seated in alphabetical order by last name. As the teacher was going through the seating chart she looked at me, looked at her chart, looked at me, looked at her chart, and finally said,

"Are you Adam?"
I said, "Yes."
"Adam Carlson?"
"Yes."
"Are you sure?"
Needless to say, I wasn't particularly pleased.

Interactions like this made me yearn for the company of more Asian Americans, so that was a big thing I looked at when I was choosing a college. I wanted to find people I could relate to, people who shared similar experiences. One of the reasons I chose Oberlin was because of its Asian/ Pacific Islander community.

At college I think people just saw me more as Adam, the guy, instead of Adam, the Asian, or as Adam, the guy who

17

did such and such, instead of Adam, the Korean. At least I'd like to think that.

My college friends knew I was adopted, but actually I don't think I was really asked about it much. But, it's always been such a large part of who I am that I automatically introduce myself as Adam Carlson, and in the same breath say, "Oh, yeah, I'm adopted from Korea." That's because people kind of look at me, with my quasi-Scandinavian name, and I know they're wondering. I tell them, "Yeah, my Dad's half Irish, half Swedish, and my Mom's all German and I'm all Korean."

I had the picture of my birth family, the one my oldest birth brother gave me, up in my dorm room and if someone asked about it, I told them. If I happened to talk to someone about being adopted, I said, "Oh yeah, I've got a picture of my birth family, would you like to see it?" A lot of people were interested, probably more intrigued by the fact that I've actually met my birth family than by the fact that I'm adopted . . . because there are a lot of people who are adopted, but not that many of them have been able to meet their birth families.

At Oberlin I didn't run into as many adoptees as I would have liked. I was involved in the Korean Students' Association, made up of mostly second-generation Koreans, or international students -- not that many adoptees, which kind of disappointed me. I think discussion with people who have had similar experiences to you is the best way to approach that subject, especially with teenagers or young adults. For a few years, my friend and I ran a group for Korean adopted teenagers in the D.C. area. Unfortunately, most of the people who were involved in the group weren't as willing to talk about adoption as we were, but I think

18

they liked the environment.

I've always felt good about my parents' openness about adoption. It's really helped me to get questions answered and helped me to be open about it myself. I don't think they ever really tried to force it on me. They didn't sit down and tell me, "Adam, you're adopted. You're from Korea. We didn't give birth to you." I just remember always feeling that I was able to ask them a question and they would always give me the best answer they could.

They were open, but passively so. Something forced would not have been good. They gave us information gradually. For instance, my dad would go through little books we had laying around and where it said "mother or father," he would cross it out and write "birthmother" or "birthfather." He did that in more than one book. He wanted to make sure we knew the difference.

I think if you start trying to educate children about their adoption when they aren't ready, then they'll just build up a wall, and it will be much harder later to break it down. It's better to let them reach the stage where they feel comfortable about learning about adoption on their own time

When it comes to the decision to search for birthparents, it depends on the individual and you can't really make a blanket statement about what is good for adoptive children. It depends on so many things more than just the fact that they're adopted. It depends on who they are, what kind of environment they've been raised in, what they think about adoption, things like that.

I've known adoptees who weren't interested at all in learning about their adoption, or about Korea, even though they grew up with parents who were open to all their questions. Some kids don't want to meet their birthparents at

19

all, some want to meet them as soon as they find out they're adopted, some might wait till they're 30. I think adoptees should make their individual rules, say what they believe, and do what they feel, what they want to, about their status as an adoptee. I think I've discovered more about myself while learning about adoption and going through the whole search process.

I identify myself as a Korean American, with an emphasis on the American in the present, but an emphasis on the Korean in the past, possibly. I'm an American because I was raised in America and America is the culture I know, but I identify my blood with Korea. I identify myself as an adoptee, first and foremost, and I think that has had the greatest influence on my life, because if I wasn't an adoptee, I wouldn't be an American.

I'm the product of loving parents and a good upper middle-class home. I've received a good education, when I've wanted to, and I think I'm very comfortable and very happy with where I am right now in my life.

Like my birthmother said, she wanted to give me the best opportunity she could . . . I believe she did.

Adam Carlson, 25
Brooklyn, New York

20

이

Ami

Apart from being the youngest in my family, I am also the only one who is adopted. My siblings, Dan, Paul, Ellen and Ted, are what some would call homemade. As for me I was found, only a week old, on a street in Chunju. After spending four years in an orphanage, I was given to the Holt adoption agency in Seoul, where I was adopted in 1975. Because they wanted another girl, my parents chose to adopt after my mother had a miscarriage and her tubes were tied. But, when I was 8, my mother divorced my father after so many years of dealing with his alcoholism. When I think about it now, I still want to believe in the happiness my parents felt when deciding to adopt me.

Throughout my childhood, I have called many places home. We first lived in a resort town in rural

21

Wisconsin where my family owned a bar. My town had 500 people, all Caucasian, I was the only person of color and also the first person of color most had ever seen in their whole entire lives.

I knew I was adopted from Korea, but I didn't know where Korea was or really anything about it. I think my parents just looked at it as raising their own child, not offering me any kind of resources about Korea or even thinking about it. Actually I didn't even really think of myself as Korean. I was just a person of color, a minority. I knew that because children would tease me every day, telling me that I was obviously different. They would call me names, like "nigger," "chink" and "Jap." They were afraid to play with me, but I was more afraid of the teasing and the humiliation. I guess I didn't want to bring those problems to my mother, just because I thought she was working so hard already. But, when I did tell her, she calmed me, saying she was my friend and that I was not alone.

I always knew I was different, but it was pretty much ignored within my family. I actually sort of denied it, too. My mother and father spelled my name Ami, and even when I was in kindergarten, I started to spell my name Amy, just because I didn't want to be different. You know, I knew I was already different so I wanted to at least spell my name the common way. Nafzger, my last name, was another problem. I couldn't even pronounce it for the first five or six years.

I remember when my uncle was getting married for the first time and I was 12 years old or whatever and I remember going to their wedding and I kept saying, "I don't want to go," and asking my mom, "Does my new aunt know that I'm a Korean, you know, that I'm a different color?" I remember every time we drove somewhere to meet someone, I always had to make sure, and be reassured, that they knew about me because I didn't want to surprise them and shock them or anything.

In high school, we moved to Wilmer, Minnesota, a bigger city with 20,000 people. It was a very wealthy little city with lots of Norwegians. It was just a lot of rich kids and I was not one of them. I dyed my hair blonde and wanted green contacts. I wanted to be very, very white to fit in with my peers and the popular people. I was involved in choir and band, activities my mother wanted me to do. She was a musician and so I did that. I liked running a lot, so I was in cross-country, track and gymnastics. Then I got really sick. I had spinal meningitis and I was in a coma for three days, so I had to quit all of my sports, I was in the hospital for about a month during Christmas time. My family was there for me . . . my brothers and sister visited.

I was an average student, I guess. My mother couldn't help me much, but I'd always ask her to. For me I always felt like I had to try doubly harder than other students who could read something once and remember it, just like that, and get an A. I felt like I had to study it two, three, four times before I could understand it. I had a hard time understanding many things when I was younger. I think it was all the turmoil in my family and also just getting my English right . . . I wasn't confident about myself. I was very insecure.

I didn't date anybody in town. There was one guy though that I did like. He lived in another small city near ours. In the end, he turned out to be not a good guy. Well, we dated for three years, for a long time. He was the first boyfriend I had, but it turned out that he always told his mother and father that I was Hawaiian even though he knew I was Korean. He thought that would be more acceptable to them. It was

23

partly my fault because I was always ashamed of who I was. Actually, he probably didn't know what Korean was and it was the same with me, because I didn't have that information myself. I didn't even know where it was on the map. I think I just didn't care.

When I was a junior in high school, my mother got cancer. When I was a senior, she became so sick I had to help her so I went to school during the day and at night I went to our community technical college to become a nursing assistant because I heard that you could make a lot of money that way. My mother told me I had to start supporting myself because she knew she wouldn't be with me very long.

At the age of 17, a month before I graduated from high school, my mom passed away. I was the only one still living at home. My brothers and sister were all at the funeral, but afterwards they went back to school or work or whatever. It was their way to escape from the whole thing, but I couldn't. No other relatives were around to help me out. My mother's brother had died a couple years earlier. I had another uncle but he lived all the way in Arizona. I hadn't seen my father since the divorce. He ended up coming to the funeral and then I saw him once a year until he died of cancer in May 1999. Some good friends of my mother let me stay in their house the summer after she died. Then I ended up moving out and I was on my own.

After my mother died, I felt very alone. When I really, really thought about it, I really didn't care anymore. I really didn't care about life. I didn't care about me because I felt like I didn't have friends. My mom had always told me that she was like my friend and I couldn't understand how a daughter and mother could be friends. Actually, I didn't understand that for the longest time until after she died and

24

then I realized, too late, that we were friends.

I really didn't care where I ended up, or anything. I could've literally ended up on the streets, but my mom had made me promise her that I'd go to Augsburg College. It's a well-respected Lutheran college in the Twin Cities and my mother and a lot of her close friends went there. That's why I told her I would go.

I got some scholarships, but the school was expensive. For the first two years, I was in the dormitory and then after that I couldn't afford too many loans, so I ended up having to work a lot. All my friends had parents who paid for their school, but I was working three jobs and going to school. That was really difficult, not being able to put all of my potential into school, even as much as I wanted to. I've always thought that was the worst time of my life. I didn't know what I wished to do. I didn't have a direction.

Unlike other places in my life, my college helped me realize my ethnicity. It was right in downtown Minneapolis, and there were a lot of Asians and African Americans. Actually, that's the first time I saw an Asian and I just ran away. I didn't know what to do. I was basically prejudiced against my own kind. After a while, I realized that and I joined the Cross-Cultural Asian Club. I was never close to anybody in college but the club really helped me identify who I was and be accepted for it. The year right after I got out of college I joined a group called Minnesota Adopted Koreans. The close friendships formed in these two groups helped me to find something lost inside me and to define my future.

I never knew anything about my birth family. My mother and father had told me everything that they knew, which was nothing. Mother, father: unknown. That's it. I actually first started to think about finding my birth family

25

when I was in high school, but I never really did anything about it. I don't know, but for some reason, I didn't feel like it because my mother and father were still alive. It didn't matter about my father so much, but I had mentioned it to my mother once and she didn't like it. I felt like I would hurt her if I searched.

In 1994, right after I graduated from college, I went to Korea for the first time and that's when I thought about it, really a lot. Two years later, when I went back to Korea to live, I definitely decided to do something. I went back to my old orphanage and they told me my Korean name was Jin Inja and that I was found in Chunju. I learned I was at a temporary orphanage for 10 days before I was sent to another one in Iksan along with 10 other babies. I stayed there until I was given to Holt.

After I placed an ad in a Korean newspaper this man came forward and thought he was my father. It was really weird because we actually looked a lot alike. There were so many similarities: same Korean name, same location, both left handed, and his son was left handed, which is obviously genetic. Everyone was so convinced that he was my father. KBS (the Korean national TV network) was even convinced. They paid for the DNA test and brought me down to film a spot. They spent so much money because they thought for sure that he was my father. But then the DNA turned out negative.

After the reunion, KBS and I went back to my old orphanage again and found out that my orphanage had actually been lying to me. First they had my name right and then it was crossed out and then they had my new name, a different name, but it too was crossed out. Then they put my first name back again. I thought that this was really odd and asked about it. They said, "No, no, we changed it; we thought it was this, but no, this is it." So, I thought this was who I was. I came from that orphanage with 10 different babies: three died; one was taken back by the father, and six babies were left. Eventually, they admitted on KBS that they mismanaged my orphan files. They said that I probably was one of those six girls, but they didn't know which one. I wondered if my name was Jin Inja. Could I be someone else?

If I wanted to, I could research it by tracing all these people. I just decided it's not really right to interrupt people's lives, their homes, to find out what happened. So, I just let it be . . . actually there is one girl, Kimberly, who's a friend of mine from Minneapolis. It's kind of ironic we're from the same place and she's one of the six girls. We're like soul sisters, though, because I mean that orphanage is very small.

I never did another search because I had done that one for two years, and that was the outcome and I figured just let it be. If someone was out there he would have been bound to see me on TV or in the media. After five years no one had come forward except that man and I never found out anything about my birthmother. I just figure it's meant to be this way, and I guess I'm very content and satisfied with knowing that I actually tried, and that's all that counts. I know if I had not tried, I would still be curious. In the process of going through the search you learn a lot about yourself and about other people. I've really grown inside and it's something I will never, ever regret.

I lived in Korea for seven years, from 1996 to 2003. All my life, I just wanted to be accepted by somebody or a group of people, and so I just thought that was the way. I felt like my life in the States was so hard and difficult, trying to support myself all the time. It's strange, but like many adoptees, I felt like I would find some belonging and acceptance in Korea.

27

Everyone is Korean, so physically you look like you belong. I felt that way for a while, but the moment you open your mouth, it's obvious you don't really belong. But in some ways, it was like the race thing was still more important than the language. You just feel more comfortable there.

During my first year there I became engaged to a Korean man, and I almost married him. When I started dating this guy, an engineer for Samsung, he was a student of mine, learning English from me. I think all my life I'd been looking for someone who would accept me and not put me down for who I was, and who wasn't ashamed to be with an Asian or Korean. He was more in a hurry than I was because his parents wanted him to marry. He was that age, and I was looking very, very vulnerable, wanting to feel like someone accepted me, you know, for the first time in my life.

We tried to live together before we would get married, although it was very hush-hush. I soon learned that Korean men totally change when you're living together. It's like he had ownership papers. He wanted me to quit my job, dress like a Korean woman, and just stay home. I couldn't see my friends or any of my past students, or anything like that. Just be a housewife, that's what he expected me to do, and it bothered me because he wouldn't even teach me the Korean language, and when I tried to speak Korean, he'd speak English back to me. Yet in other ways, he expected me to be very Korean because he wanted me to stay home and wouldn't let me go out. I wasn't happy. I didn't have my own life.

His mother hated me and she would hit me a lot. I didn't know what to do. I didn't understand a word she was saying to me. His father really liked me a lot, and I'm not sure why, but he really liked me. I don't think either the father or my fiancé realized how the mother treated me. Why did she act like that? For one reason, I think the mother obviously expected that her son would marry someone she could communicate with. Another problem was my being an adoptee . . . in Korea, they're very ashamed of that, but the father, for some reason, accepted me.

It was difficult to break off the relationship because he was more concerned about just being married, the status of being married, because of his age. Well, he wasn't that old, only about one year older than I and I was 27 at that time, but he didn't want to look for another girl to get married to. Living together was like a hush-hush thing, more like a marriage in Korea.

Our relationship lasted about one year. It just came down to the fact that he was not friendly towards me. He was drunk. I'd have to go pick him up in the middle of night, at 3 or 4 a.m. He didn't care about me. He cared all about the image. He'd do his own thing -- drink every night with the guys, his co-workers. I learned a lot about Korean culture very fast. Then, he started to beat me up and I left him. In college I had taken the social work course and that helped me out a lot. I did an article on Korean women being battered, so I knew right then I had to get out. I got in the relationship mostly to find acceptance with myself and understand my issues. It was part of the same reason I went into social work.

I had a lot of anger built up at the time, but now that's gone. We were not right for each other. We were of different cultures. He did call me later and we mutually decided to be friends. He apologized for everything, realized how he was and that he couldn't change me.

Looking back, I remember being very ashamed when I first went to Korea. For a while I was actually extremely

29

ashamed because I didn't know how to read or speak Korean and I didn't know how to use chopsticks. But I wasn't ashamed about being an adoptee. I was ashamed because I was Korean blood, and I didn't know anything about Korea. It was apparent to the Koreans that I was not one of them, and they did everything possible to reinforce this idea. They went as far as to bluntly tell me to my face that I was a foreigner. The Koreans I came across had pity on me because I was an adoptee, and that really bothered me.

I guess when I was there, I felt very responsible for not knowing about Korea. The first thing I tried to do was to tell Koreans why I didn't know, but their first remark still was, "Well, you should know, you should learn how to speak Korean, you should learn how to do this." But, when nobody gives you the opportunity to learn or to be able to go to school to study the language, it's very hard and that's probably what's so frustrating. You want them to encourage you, to say, "I can help you, or I would like to help you." Many of them do say that, but they never follow through.

I originally was going to go to Korea for two years, just to learn about Korean culture. If I would have been teaching English the whole time, I would have probably left Korea right away. But I had this chance to work with the organization Global Overseas Adoptees' Link (G.O.A.'L), so that's what kind of encouraged me to stay longer. I felt like I was actually doing something, making a difference. I was trying to make the adoptees' voices heard. I think my major goal when we first started was more like having a support group, but somehow I got the attention of the media through my Korean friends, and it was the domino effect -- some of my Korean friends helped, and the media did a story, and then more Koreans wanted to help. Then some adoptees found out . . . it just happened so fast.

After the first six months, I started realizing that I was doing so much for adoptees. I was picking them up at the airport and they would stay at my house. I would just talk to them a lot about Koreans, teach them the subway, all the small nuts and bolts about survival in Korea. The more I did that, the word spread very fast. Then we started to arrange home stays and searches, just everything, so it got big very fast. We also did a lot of stuff for the Korean community, businesses and society, for a lot of people, not just adoptees. G.O.A.'L now receives scholarships through the universities, and we offer them to adoptees to learn Korean. It's something I wish I could have had. G.O.A.'L is now a home base for adult adoptees returning to Korea. It tries to build mutual respect between adoptees and Koreans, to bridge the gap between the two cultures. That's the reputation we have now.

During my years in Korea, I met so many adoptees who had troubles similar to mine. Many in my generation of adoptees did not have proper placements. In our conversations, thinking about suicide was a common theme. It's frightening but I do know adoptees who've carried it out. We also talked about our identity and how we felt about not belonging to either our adoptive country or our birth countries and how our lives were without direction and without Korean role models. It was nice to be able to get together and give support. There were a number of European adoptees that I became close to.

In 2002, before I left, I wanted to make sure G.O.A.'L was stable. At the time there was a staff of five and about 1000 volunteers registered with G.O.A.'L. It felt very good to have this strong following. It was very hard to actually let it all go . . . all my sweat and time I had spent fulfilling

31

this passionate goal, and I let it go to people that I trained but hardly knew. I felt a sense of loss when I got back to America. It was kind of different not to have so many people depend on me. I knew it was something I had to let go of someday, and I figured that was the time. I felt I was still kind of young and that I could start another career. Although I have left, I still act as an executive advisor for G.O.A.'L. They ask for my help in publicizing G.O.A.'L's efforts and mission here in the U.S. Hopefully one day I can make it into a nonprofit here, so there can be funds raised and sent back to Korea.

I really miss the passion I had at G.O.A.'L, having a purpose, making a difference, and helping people. It's something I don't have here as much. Still, I have taken an active role on the board of directors for the nonprofit Asian Pacific Cultural Center here in Minnesota. It's taken years to get funding, but we're expecting to open our Pan-Asian Center by 2008.

Through my struggles, I have become a very strong person. I know what I want, and I know more about myself. I'm very, very confident and proud of being an Asian, and very confident and proud of knowing the Korean culture. I don't just consider myself a Korean, but rather I'm a Korean who knows the culture and my history. That's what makes me proud. My journey to Korea has really, really helped me have confidence in my identity. I know for a fact that if I had never gone to Korea, I would not feel this way. I mean I'd still probably be having some of these questions or curiosities. My journey there has helped my longing . . . has helped me to actually be proud.

When I look at myself, I see a Korean-American adoptee. I do not see that I am only a Korean American. Korean

32

Americans are very different, by upbringing and by belief. I am a Korean-American adoptee, that's how I define myself. I'm not ashamed of it. I'm proud. I feel like I can, you know, teach many people so many things.

Ami Nafzger, 35
Workforce Development Manager
Goodwill Easter Seals
Founder and President,
Global Overseas Adoptees' Link (G.O.A.'L) USA
Minneapolis, Minnesota

삼

Michelle

I was actually 5 months old when I was adopted. For three years it was just my mom, my dad and I, and then they adopted my brother Joey from Pusan, Korea when he was 9 months old. A couple months after they got him, my parents found out that Joey was mentally challenged. He has an IQ maybe of 40. I believe that when my mom asked the adoption agency why they weren't told about the problem, the agency claimed not to have known. My mom took him to the doctor because he wasn't responsive as most babies and wasn't making little baby noises, or even trying to walk. I think the agency actually offered to take him back. I guess it's the only thing they could have done, but it's kind of sad, you know, we'll take the kid back if you're not happy with him.

35

I'm glad my parents kept him because he's the best kid ever, really sweet.

When I was close to 4, my parents divorced. So, for most of the time when I was growing up, I lived with my mom and brother in a suburban neighborhood in Wilmington, Delaware, a nice, safe community with working families. My father stayed in the house my parents had built together in a wealthier, wooded area. He remarried when I was 7 or 8. My relationship with him weakened during college and I really have no desire to see him. My mother has stayed single.

I don't remember an exact moment when I realized I was different from my family and friends. It was just something my parents tried to instill in me, even as a baby . . . it's not something you can really deny a kid, so they would tell me about it when I was younger. My mom's told me stories about holding me in front of a mirror with her and pointing, doing that whole thing that people do with little kids.

When I was younger, my mom tried to give me contact with other Koreans, taking me to the Korean community center in Philadelphia. I don't remember any of that, but I'm sure I knew what these people looked like and what I looked like. My parents would take me out to eat Korean or Japanese food and to Korean grocery stores . . . I guess just so I could see other people like me. I wouldn't say I had a whole lot of exposure to other Asians and they never said they were doing these things specifically because of me, but I guess I knew they probably wouldn't have done it had I not been there.

I never met any of my mom's family, but my dad's family's pretty big, so I saw my grandparents on a regular basis and my aunts and my uncles fairly often. It really didn't matter that I was different. I mean family's family and

36

it was never a topic of discussion. My friends were mostly Caucasian. From first through sixth grade, I went to a very small private school, probably only about 25-30 kids in my grade, mostly kids who came from wealthier Caucasian families.

I wasn't the only minority child. There was another kid -- Chinese, I believe -- but he skipped a couple of grades and I don't know what happened to him. I don't really think I was conscious of being different when I was really young, like 5 or 6, but it became more noticeable to me as I grew up. At school there were different expectations. Little kids just kind of say whatever they're thinking, and kids would think oh, because she's Asian, she's good in math and really smart. You get really sick of that after a while. True or not, you get sick of that.

I tried to ignore it for a while. I can remember wanting to get plastic surgery on my eyes and my nose so I'd look like my mom. I didn't want to go out and eat Korean food anymore. My mom would try to take me to Korean activities at the Chinese community center down the street, and I just didn't want to go. When I was younger, I'm sure I asked questions about my adoption and Korea . . . all little kids ask questions. As I got older, I think I stopped, but I don't necessarily know why. It wasn't a lack of positive feedback or anything. I just wasn't really interested. My mom was always very helpful. If I asked her a question, she would do her best to answer it. If she didn't know the answer, she was honest and told me.

Maybe it was that it felt kind of silly going to Korean restaurants and such, but it's really hard to know. There's really no right way to go about something like that. It all depends on the kid. I don't remember a whole lot of how I

37

felt before age 9, but as I started to reach adolescence I was aware of being different and then I would try to ignore it or deny it for awhile because there are so many stereotypes that go along with it. It's the first thing that people see when they look at you . . . you are, I guess, a foreigner or something. I mean I wasn't really that foreign. I was born in Korea, but raised in America, but how you look is what people perceive when they first are in contact with you. I knew I didn't look Caucasian like the majority, but I handled it by ignoring it.

My mom didn't think this was very healthy for me. I guess it got to the point where my mom just wanted me to deal with it and she got me to Camp Sejong. I don't even remember how she heard about it really. I was the only kid from Delaware. It was based in northern New Jersey where there's a pretty big population of Korean Americans, so I went up there and it was a great experience, the best thing that ever could have happened to me.

The counselors were all college students, and I think the majority of them were actually from Korean families, maybe only one or two adoptees like me. The role models there were really great . . . I was what, like 11 or 12, and these camp counselors were really cool, probably like 18 or 19. They were all going to great schools and doing really well. They all knew so much about their heritage. I made really good friends at camp and I still keep in touch with them by phone and e-mail, even though they all live really far away.

It was just really enlightening. I'd never been someplace where there were so many Korean people and also so many kids who were like me, adopted as well. There was a social worker there, Deborah Johnson from Minnesota. That was the first time I really felt okay to talk about issues about adoption, maybe the first time I really wanted to. It was good to have people who understood or felt similar feelings about being adopted and not always wanting to be Asian, maybe wanting to be white or Caucasian, or whatever you want to call it, for a little while. We talked about maybe wanting to find our birthparents, what kind of discrimination we faced, and then with my peers, we all came up with ways to deal with it. It was a really nice support system.

I really can't explain the difference between camp and when my mom had tried to get me to go to other support groups. I guess at camp I felt like I didn't have my mom watching over my back. I wouldn't have to go home to my mom and tell her what I did. I got to spend a whole week at overnight camp with all these people, and we got to eat Korean food, learn some Korean songs and prayers. For lack of better words, I was very inspired to learn more about the country that gave me birth.

That fall I went to a parade up in New York City for Choosok (a day of thanksgiving to honor ancestors). The camp counselors and the lady who was in charge of the camp let us all know that this was a huge parade, telling us, "You guys are more than welcome to come, we're going to be in it." So I went up and I had a really great time, and I got to see some of my friends again.

I was really inspired to learn more about the country that I came from, and I believe it was around that time or maybe the next year that an adoptive families' support group asked me to come and represent Korea, talk to some parents and some kids. I made some posters, and I got some pamphlets together about things I had learned at camp. When I got back, I just had this desire to learn more. That's what drove me to go to Korean school for two years. I was actually the first adopted kid to go. Most of the kids there came from Korean families, so they could practice their Korean at home. There were some 6-year-old kids who knew more Korean than the 12-year-olds. It all depended on how the parents had tried to get them to learn Korean when they were younger. I think I was the oldest at the time.

Eventually I started working by myself with this one teacher. She was really great. Actually, it's kind of funny. I saw her on the University of Delaware campus when I was a student there. I think she teaches Japanese. She was a really smart lady, and she made me feel really good about what I was doing, the progress I was making, because she tried to sympathize with me. Learning another language is s-o-o hard especially when you start when you're older. You have to learn a whole new alphabet, and I didn't have anywhere to practice it. I couldn't practice it at home, and I didn't really hang out with any kids from a Korean background so it was really hard, but I felt really encouraged. When I went into high school, I just had less and less time to do it, and now I can understand very little, just the basics. If I go out to eat Korean, I know how to be polite and how to greet people.

Starting in seventh grade, I went to Ursuline Academy, an all-girls' Catholic school. I wouldn't say it was a very good experience. I didn't like the superficiality of all the girls. My parents didn't have any religion that they raised me with so I got really sick of that really quick. It was the summer before I started that I had gone to Camp Sejong, so I had a different attitude about my Korean identity when I went to Ursuline, a more positive, open and active attitude. I faced some stereotypes or generalizations, but I don't think it was bad.

There was a boys' Catholic school down the road and I

dated on and off in high school. I don't really think my being adopted or Korean mattered to my dates. I've asked boys what they thought about it, and I guess the most common response was that it wasn't a problem at all. They said, "You're Michelle, that's all, and Michelle is Korean, but you are still Michelle." That's why I was friends with them. The guy I'm dating now is Caucasian. I met him in high school and he also went to Delaware with me. I asked him about it and he was like, "It doesn't really matter, we get to go out and eat Korean food. I mean it's not anything really worth discussing." I just asked because it was my birthday and I was thinking more about my birthmother -- and about Korea.

Every now and then my adoption and being Korean will come up and I'll think about it for a couple of weeks. Then I'll forget about it and concentrate on school and other stuff and I'll come back to it. It comes in spurts I guess.

I just wonder about my birthmom, wonder if she's okay, wonder if she would be proud of me right now, wonder what she's doing. I don't know anything about her. For some reason, my mom told me that my birthmother was very young and unmarried when she had me. I never asked her why she said that. I would guess she's now probably in her late 30s. Wow! That's really young for a mother to have a daughter my age, but that's how old I assume she is and how old I've always thought of her as.

When I was maybe 17 or 18, I remember thinking I'm probably as old as my birthmom was when she had me. I remember thinking about that and it being really creepy. I have friends who are getting married and I have a friend who has a kid, and they're my age and it's just, I'm nowhere near any of that.

I went to Korea the summer before my senior year in

high school with a group of kids from Camp Sejong and some young adult Korean adoptees. We were sponsored by a group of businessmen trying to build a bridge between America and South Korea. We were there for nine days and it was the coolest experience ever. I had a great time, but I always describe it as a very bittersweet experience . . . such a beautiful country, but it kind of hurt that a country that beautiful had to give me up for adoption. In a way, I just felt Korea had rejected me. From a really long time back I can remember resenting the people who couldn't take care of me -- the country that seemingly didn't want me and my little brother and my friends from camp.

In Korea everyone that we met, that we stayed with, that we talked to, everyone was really, really nice. The culture was beautiful, and it's something that when I got there, I realized that this whole time, deep down, I was judging this country for not wanting me, but in a way I couldn't. It wasn't fair for me to do that, it wasn't fair for me to be upset at a country that didn't take care of me. It wasn't that they couldn't, that they didn't, that anyone didn't want to, or even the whole country didn't want to, because I realized it wasn't fair . . . because them not taking care of me and their beautiful culture were two completely different things.

When I tell people about my trip to Korea, I get so happy because Korea is so beautiful. It's hard to believe that it's on the same planet as Delaware, as the rest of America, but I just remember thinking that the land has so much history. You can see the history in the land, and here you don't. You see big buildings and big statues, and there are mountains and stuff, but there's nothing here in America that's just so old like in Korea.

When I was there I definitely felt like an outsider most of

42

the time, like a tourist. I felt more American than ever. When I was with the larger group, I was like, everyone's looking at us, they know we're American, because there must have been 30 of us, walking around together, riding this big bus.

But I can remember walking down the street in Seoul with some of my friends and we weren't with any older people. It was just us. I think we were shopping and it was really neat. I fit in. I was in the majority and I wasn't that foreign face anymore. I looked like everybody else. I felt like I was Korean, even though my little secret was that I was American. It was a very new feeling, kind of scary at first, but still great, and I can't think of anything that has ever even come close to matching it.

I haven't felt it since because I think that despite the presence of Asians in America, even for so many years, people here still see Asian, and, when they look at me, they still see a foreign face. Even for Asians born here, the same thing happens. In Korea, even if people looked at me, I didn't think it was because I was Asian, but probably because I can be goofy looking.

Second glances are something I'm pretty used to. I got my lower lip pierced when I was 18 and I have pretty large breasts for an Asian. That just surprises the hell out of people sometimes. When I was in Korea, I was getting measured for my hanbok that I was going to wear to see the Korean president. This little Korean lady was taking my measurements and she actually grabbed my chest to see if it was real. It was really funny because her head was probably up to my chin -- she was so tiny. I was in the middle of a conversation at this point, and I just kind of looked at her for a second. It was definitely funnier afterwards. Even I'm surprised that they're so big.

43

My goofy look is something that started in high school. I wasn't matching with the other girls in my small Catholic school. There were, I think, 44, 45 girls in my graduating class and all I knew from the time I got there was that I did not want to be like them. I was already different and I made myself even more different. I have found it's something for me to revel in almost.

When I was 16 I got my Korean tattoo on my lower back, and now I'm in the middle of a bigger tattoo, kind of like a collage, on my upper right shoulder. It started small -- with my Korean name and the Chinese character for stars. Whenever I get money, whenever I win the lottery, I plan on finishing the collage and it's going to be like my spot for my birthmom. I got the idea from something my mother told me when I was little. She would always say that no matter where I was, I was always under the same stars as my birthmom. It's kinda goofy but, when I was at camp, I had a friend there who had an incredible voice. She sang this song from the movie *American Tail* where this little mouse Feivel is separated from his family, and he's so sad . . . he must be like a little kid-mouse and he sits by the window and sings, "Somewhere out there, beneath the pale blue sky." I don't even remember all the words, but it has to do with being under the same stars as someone you really care for.

When I was younger I was more angry about my adoption, but I've come to understand that sometimes people just have to do stuff that they don't necessarily want to do, or sometimes they do stuff that hurts. Even though my mom was always very sympathetic when we would talk about it, I still didn't really have a good relationship with her when I was 12, 13 and 14. I don't think it was necessarily because I was struggling with part of my identity. Sometimes I think

44

I was just a mess in general. Maybe if my mom had sent me to Camp Sejong earlier things could have been different, but I can't necessarily attribute the relationship quality to any one thing. It may have been because I was just maturing. At that age, she wanted to support me more but this was something that she didn't know anything about . . . there was no way she could know what I was feeling or going through. She just tried to support me as best that she could. Now we have more of a friendship as opposed to a mother-daughter relationship. She just wants to share more about herself and her personal experiences to help me.

I just would like to meet my birthmother . . . to show her that I turned out well. I've put my information into a couple databases that help adoptees find their birthparents, but I haven't heard anything. My adoption papers and my birth papers are all pretty blank, so I really don't have much to offer except a case number, a birth date, April 14, 1982, the name of the orphanage, and stuff like that.

I was probably 15 or 16 when I started thinking about getting my birth records. I just have this funny feeling that I still don't have what was really there. I've been told, just by various people that it's hard, really hard to get your records, the real records from Korea. I've looked at what I have time and time again, and there's nothing about my birthmother, her family or her biological history. It says nothing about her except that she was Korean.

I've tried to get a copy of my records from the agency here to see if there is any more information from the American side of the adoption and they said I have everything that's in my file, etc., etc. It actually says in my records somewhere that they tried to contact my birthmother, and they sent her a letter, but the letter was sent back. It turned out that the address

45

and name were false. I've gone over it like a thousand times. Why don't I have a copy of that letter? If I have everything in my file, then why don't I have that? Even though I think the records about my birthmother are erroneous, I haven't done much more research. It's like $100 to get your records translated or whatever. As much as I want something like that, I have my doubts if I'm actually ready for it.

Asking for my records was all something I did on my own, with my mom's support. She's always been really supportive, and I appreciate that. I know that some parents aren't, I mean they're afraid that their kids are going to go live with their birthparents. My mom helped me get any information I could. But, she always wanted it to be my decision, didn't want me to feel pressured into doing it. At the same time, she didn't want me to miss out on any opportunity. When I went to Korea, I think they offered the older people on the trip, over 18 or 20 or something, the opportunity to have Korean officials of some sort look into their family history or their adoption agency. I remember being 16, just so young, so I wasn't old enough.

When I look for role models, I think I'd like to be like my birthmother, really strong. I have this big story in my mind about what happened to my birthmom. I mean when she was pregnant with me, it wasn't very socially acceptable, being that she wasn't married. I know that sometimes women get shipped off to convents or places for women who aren't married, have their kids, and then come back into society. I have a vague idea that something like that happened to my birthmom and it was really hard for her. I'd like to be able to deal with things like her, be as strong as she was.

At one time in their lives, I think all adopted kids fantasize about what their birthparents were like, what they went through. I don't know what my birthmom went through. I don't know a lot about Korea, but my understanding is that unwed pregnancies, teenage pregnancies, are more taboo in Korea than they are here. To go through what she did, you have to be very, very strong.

Although my mother and I speculate that my birthmother was really young, for all we know she could have been 30 and already had too many kids. But in my mind, the picture I've painted was that she was very young and at a point in her life where she couldn't take care of a baby. She wanted the baby to have a better life, and I think that is a very selfless act.

Obviously she was a strong and wonderful woman. I mean, she didn't just leave me anywhere . . . she left me in a hospital. She didn't abort me . . . she left me somewhere where I would be cared for. I think it was called the Angels Hospital in Seoul. I have no idea of anything about her. I just know that she went to this big city and she took me somewhere where she knew I would be cared for. I mean women in America can't even do that. Women leave their kids all over the place here. It's crazy.

I hardly ever think about my birthfather. I couldn't tell you why. He was just as much a part of it, but I guess it was just the thing about her carrying me for nine months, carrying me inside of her and leaving me somewhere very important.

Every time my birthday comes around I think about her. I just wonder if she remembers, if she thinks about me or what she thinks about . . . thousands of things run through my head about what kinds of things she thinks about. When I was in Korea, I had those kinds of thoughts a lot.

Several years ago, for my college entrance essay, I wrote a letter to my birthmother. At first all the topic choices seemed very vague. I finally decided on the one option that was to write about something that was really important to me, something that would reflect who I was and that played a very significant role in my life. I'm really proud of what I wrote:

Dear _____,

I don't know what to call you, and I don't know exactly where you are in this world. I do know, however, that part of you is with me. I see your reflection in my eyes. I hear your voice when I sing. I cry your tears when I cry. You are in my thoughts, yet I have no realistic pictures in my mind. I can only hope that you are safe and doing well in your unknown place.

You pervade my soul daily. I strive for excellence so that one day I may show you my accomplishments and make you proud of me. Your strength carries me as I surge to conquer my demons. I overcome humiliation by searching deep within me to find my inner pride. Most of all, I have found that sacrificing my desires and facing my fears are necessary parts of love.

My sorrows and frustrations are not forgotten. These feelings haunt and betray me. They connect me to you, sometimes taking on a life of my own, disconnecting me from myself. I am often forced to take steps backwards in my journey to self-identity because of knowledge I lack.

You left me in a place with unknown consequences, so I could be taken somewhere better. Your loss in this life was for mine to have hope. We parallel each other yet we are worlds apart.

Your birth daughter, Your Seoul baby,
Michelle Zebrowski, Sung Sin Lee

Michelle Zebrowski, 25
B.A. in philosophy,
University of Delaware

Todd

I was 2 years old when I was adopted early in 1976 by a Caucasian family. My mother and father already had two children of their own, a 6-year-old daughter and a 5-year-old son. I guess adopting me was something they either wanted to do or were called to do since a lot of Christian families adopt. I'm not sure why, perhaps they merely wanted some diversity in their lives.

My parents never really talked much to me about my adoption. Before I came they talked about it a lot with my siblings, I guess, trying to get them acquainted with the idea of having another brother from a different country. It turns out my brother and sister were really excited to have me. I think my parents must have coached them well.

51

I was raised in rural, southern Maryland, a community mostly of whites and blacks in an area with a naval base and lots of strip malls. My father still has his dental practice there, and my mother is a public health coordinator. My family attended an Episcopal church, which really accepted me and brought me in from day one. I was a big deal for my church community.

I don't remember too much about the years right after my adoption. I do remember going to Montessori school and as a kid, being very hard to deal with sometimes. I threw a lot of tantrums, daily tantrums for a long time. That's what I can remember. Nothing I'm very proud of, but knowing that I was a child forced into a different environment, I think the tantrums were a natural thing, just a feeling of loss. I wasn't really that bad, but anything could set me off, especially not getting what I wanted. It got to a point where my mother knew a tantrum was coming. It was almost a scheduled event. I think it was hard for my siblings, but that's what happened.

My mother was always the strict one, the enforcer, while my father was a gentler, more laid-back guy. As any parent would, I was sent to my room a lot, put in time-out and spanked. That was a normal occurrence. I'm sure my parents had an inkling that the tantrums had something to do with my adoption, but I think they probably just thought they could deal with it or it would eventually settle down and things would change. But, the tantrums continued throughout my childhood.

I would feel just rage, pure rage, pure anger. It must have stemmed from being abandoned or rejected or isolated. I was angry that I was adopted, but I was too young to have the ability to articulate that to my adoptive family. I was angry

52

and sad, but both feelings came across as anger. I still have a quick temper . . . still struggle with that, but from what I'm told, and I often laugh when someone talks about it, that kind of temper is inherent in most Korean men. That's something I'm kind of looking at . . . I think everyone looks at their personal qualities as they grow older and mature.

In my family we never really talked about my being Korean. It wasn't necessary because I always knew. I mean . . . I look Korean and they don't, so it was pretty obvious to me. I always felt different, knew I was different, but at the same time felt like any other kid, too. I don't want to paint a picture like I had this horrible, traumatic childhood. Aside from the tantrums, I had a pretty successful childhood.

I was always good in school, not a great tester, but I was always at the top of my class, all the way through high school. I was in the top 5 percent of my senior class, got a 3.9 grade point average. I think being a model student was more related to the family I was raised in . . . high expectations. My mother is part German and came from a disciplined background . . . you're going to be obedient and you're going to do things right, especially in education. Being so strict and conservative, that's pretty Korean, too. I've made the joke that my family was probably more Korean than they were anything else because when I talk to my Korean friends, it sounds like they experienced the same thing. Some things cross over the racial barrier.

I think I was pretty well behaved in school. I never got in trouble, but I did get picked on a lot. Kids are pretty cruel. They called me "slanted-eye," "gook," "chink," "flat-face," anything. I guess it set me apart. It just hurt because I thought I was just like the rest of them. I knew I didn't look like everybody else, but I felt like one of them.

53

The teasing singled me out. I felt embarrassed again to be who I was, and to look the way I did. If I had said something to my parents, they would have gone and talked to the principal or to the teacher and I would have looked like this little baby in class, amongst my peers, and that's certainly not the image I had or wanted. I was a tough athlete and I didn't want my mom coming out to rescue me just because kids were being mean. That would have been too embarrassing, so I never said anything to my parents. I'm glad I didn't but I do wish I'd gotten into a few fights. I think that would have done me some good, but I avoided fights because I grew up in a Christian family and was taught to turn the other cheek.

My parents really had no understanding of what an international child had to go through in a school setting, even in a social setting. They saw me at church and at home. Those are two places where I wasn't going to experience any negativity from others. I tell my mom about it now and she says, "Why didn't you ever tell us?" But, I don't think there's anything they could've or would've done. Looking back, I think it was good . . . taught me some self-control. I just dealt with it and I think it made me tough, strong.

I really don't question how my parents raised me. They would have done the same thing if my brother or sister had been teased. I have to give them a lot of credit for treating us all equally. I never felt second class and when it came to my family, I never even felt different. I just felt like the youngest, always left out, not old enough to do this, not old enough to do that. That's common, I think. My sister and brother were very sensitive to me and didn't tease me. I think my parents raised all three of us with really good values. I get along with both my siblings now, but I couldn't always

54

say that about my sister. We were -- and still are -- just very different.

Growing up in a rural area, I really didn't have any contact with Koreans or other Asians. My parents never tried to bring Korean influences into my upbringing. We had Chinese food, maybe once a year, never had a bowl of rice. I don't know if they purposely did that or not, but their intentions were always to make me feel like the rest of the kids. I don't know if they were saying, "You have to fit into our family." I think it was more a way of saying, "You're no different." As an adult, I think I kind of appreciate that now. I think if they had tried to bring Korean influences into my life, I would have rejected it. I mean, in my head I would have been thinking, you guys are phony so don't even try. It'd be like a bunch of white folks trying to teach you how to be Korean, which is a ridiculous concept. The resources now are so much better. My parents never knew that there were culture camps going on. I think if they did, they would have sent me, but I would have had a really hard time with that. It would have felt like the reverse of being adopted here, almost like being adopted again, back into Korean culture. Like most Koreans or people in general, I'm very stubborn and I have a lot of pride. I don't like to be embarrassed and I don't like to feel different. Once I made that conversion to American culture, trying to make another conversion to learn about my own culture would have seemed forced. I think it was much better for me to learn about my Korean culture on my own, as an adult.

Adoptees raised in areas like New York City or California don't really have the experience and the phases that I've described. They have Asian -- and multicultural -- influences from the beginning. If you have a cultural day, say,

55

celebrating Filipinos in New York City, big deal. But if you have a day like that in a little country town, it's kind of like, what the heck is going on? What I'm saying is that trying to bring Korean culture to where I grew up would have been phony. It wouldn't have been authentic and I'm someone that's always searching for the truth.

My mother had one friend, whom she spoke to maybe once a year, who was Korean, but I never really had any interaction. I vaguely remember going over to a Korean woman's home in our neighborhood. I just remember having to wear special slippers in her home, since shoes weren't allowed. There was also another couple, friends of my parents, who adopted a Korean girl at the same time as I was adopted. Actually we flew over together, but I didn't grow up knowing her because our families didn't socialize after adopting us. We went to different schools and she was younger than me. In hindsight, I wish I had built a friendship with her, but . . .

I called her, one time, many years ago because I felt like I had this adoptee connection with her. She seemed to be fine, but when I expressed my ideas of thinking about being adopted and searching, I don't think she had any interest in it. I don't know and I guess for her, it was never an issue since she had assimilated so well. Many adoptees, I've heard, don't get interested in searching until they have their own children. It may be a part of going full circle.

Not surprisingly, my first real interaction with Koreans didn't happen until college. My small high school had been too constricting so I chose a large university, the University of Maryland, because I wanted to go somewhere with people from every walk of life. I soon discovered that in universities people tend to hang out with their own kind. I can see how it's necessary, but diversity ended up being a synonym for segregation. In college, I started hanging out with some Koreans, opening a whole different door to my life. They were Korean Americans, but they all had Korean families and spoke Korean. When it came to fitting in with them I felt like I did, but it didn't always work.

Initially I knew nothing about Koreans or Asian people in general. I was very much intimidated by them. I didn't know how to act. I think I'd already taken on the feeling that they were all foreigners, all aliens -- the same way many Caucasian people feel if they're not exposed to other races. Once I got over that hump I think it was more just a battle of being accepted within the Asian community. I was always cautious, thinking whether or not they were going to look at me strangely. I stuck out like a sore thumb. My mannerisms were different. I dressed differently. I think Asians, or more specifically, Koreans, have their own pop culture and I didn't have a clue.

When I got to college I said I was adopted, right off the bat. I would always bring it up -- even today -- because, I mean, there's no hiding. It doesn't bother me, but once they hear my last name, people always ask uncomfortable questions. Actually, in college, it wasn't just because of my name. It was just so obvious that I was ignorant of the Korean culture. Ironically, I think I was labeled as the "white" Todd, even though there was another Todd my friends knew who actually was Caucasian. Now, except for my last name, I don't think anyone could tell that I wasn't "total Korean," maybe even from a Korean family that was pretty much very assimilated here. The only way people can tell now is when they try to speak Korean to me. In time, I was able to successfully assimilate to both cultures.

One of the key things that really molded everything and helped shape my identity was dating. With dating, you have to, you want to, be like whomever you're attracted to and that happens with any human being, adopted or not. In college, you see people going toward different music scenes, or liking similar hobbies, and you can see their identities shaping. I don't think it's strictly an adoption thing.

I didn't date at all really in high school. I could have had dates because a lot of my friends viewed me as just like them, not as being Korean. They didn't have any other Korean friends, so they had nothing to compare me to. But, I came from a very conservative, strict family so dating would have been a big deal. They didn't prohibit it. It was just that I don't think I was ready.

So I started dating, Asians in particular, in my sophomore year in college. I was very naive. The first girl I dated was Korean American and I think I was infatuated with the fact that she was Korean. I was only hurting myself because she wasn't the type of person I wanted to be with. I had grown attached for the wrong reasons and eventually understood that, but I went through a lot of different emotions during that time. I felt like I was filling part of a void by dating someone of my own ethnicity. I would point the blame to myself in situations rather than look at the other person for who they were . . . I never felt good enough . . . I had three girlfriends in college, and with each one that void was an issue. I was using the fact that they were Asian females because I never had an Asian female figure in my life, ever . . . I felt like I was learning more about myself by being with them. Certainly that wasn't the right thing to do, but I had to do it, whether I liked it or not. The relationships ended in heartbreak and depression for me, whether the break-up was mutual, I ended it, or they ended it. It was just the feeling of loss and the feeling of being rejected again by an Asian female. I wrote a poem about that void, about how I place my relationships in that predicament, putting the pressures of perhaps acceptance from a mother figure on a girlfriend. That truly was one of the biggest epiphanies I have had in the last eight years. Now I have a new girlfriend who's Asian American. Before I was so emotional in relationships, and now I'm getting feedback like, "You're so stoic," and I think that's me, protecting myself and looking at lessons learned in the past. I'm not sure where this relationship is going to go.

I think I've always wanted to search for my birth family, but it took a long time to have the courage. They've always been in my consciousness, and I've always wondered: Who are they, what are they doing, and have they thought about me? This feeling really did come from the depth of my being. There wasn't a lot of dialogue about my adoption when I was growing up. My parents were always real with me. They said they would never hold any information back, but their stand was, "We're ignorant to the facts, we don't know, so we can't really help you."

Being told that there was no information and I wasn't going to find anything -- that was basically what I heard. A lot of that was my parents trying to protect me from emotionally being hurt if I didn't find something. I think my folks always said, "You really don't have any information, we don't have any information, and you can't change it." I guess I never believed it and I'd always think to myself, you guys don't know what you're talking about at all. I had a very cocky attitude about it. I've always been the person who felt that I could change anything, accomplish anything. It's not really arrogance. It's just how I am. I guess it's pretty American to never take no for an answer. My parents just thought it'd be very difficult, but their attitude was: Accept what you are now and don't dwell on the things you cannot change.

I also think they were caring. They knew that it meant something to me, too, so it wasn't just like, "Get over it." I think I can understand that if you're adoptive parents, you don't want to tell your kids, "Yeah, your birthparents are out there thinking about you all the time." It was always kind of drilled in my head that I was given up out of love, that nobody knew the reasons why, but my birthparents must have been really poor, really been struggling to make a decision to give up a child, their own child. My parents always told me my family loved me when they gave me up. I always questioned that. I was like, "How do you know? How do you know I was loved?" And it was something my mom says she always felt, which I respect. But there are some things I've always felt, too -- that I always knew I wanted to find out more.

Approaching adulthood, I think I was driven to find answers, because things were just not working out the way I wanted. I'd get very frustrated. I felt very much a void in my life that I couldn't explain, like there was something always itching me. I really couldn't explain my frustration and my loneliness, but I always knew that it had something to do with being adopted. To be able to address that emptiness by searching was just very scary because who knows what you're going to find. Either you're opening the door to two loving arms or to a lot of potential bad situations. I lived with that scared feeling for a long time.

Along with having that feeling, I've always had the feeling that I needed to search. I mean it felt like some other force had control and whether I liked it or not, I was there

60

for the ride. I was going to do the search, and I was going to find them. I had choice in the matter, but I almost felt like I didn't. It was a matter of survival. If I wanted to survive as a human being and be happy and live a decent life, this was something I had to do. That's why it happened.

I always knew what was supposedly my name and birth date. But, when I was about 25, I really questioned even this information because I spoke with other people who were adopted and found out that a lot of their information was false, just contrived by the agencies to protect the birthparents. It really was to protect the adults, rather than the children, which is kind of sad, but I think that's changing.

I started my search mainly through the Internet. There are a lot of individuals out there who have websites and discussion boards where you can just post things, read others' postings and reply. Other adoptees tell you how they searched and what they found, negative or positive. I did a lot of that, kind of double-checking whether or not this was something I was ready to do, whether I was prepared to search and find nothing, or search and find something horrible. There are a lot of different dynamics.

I tried to read others' experiences and study as much as I could about what kind of questions you need to ask yourself. I discovered a huge adoptee network out there, a huge community. So I corresponded with them, people my age, actually making friendships, meeting people. It was pure networking, getting opportunities to participate in conferences. Obviously these had been going on for quite some time, but I had just gotten keyed into it.

The "Gathering," which was the first Korean Adoptee conference to ever occur, was held conveniently in Washington, D.C. which, I guess, was pretty pivotal. For

61

me, it wasn't so much a search for my identity . . . it was just making the right connections, and I ended up contacting G.O.A.'L (Global Overseas Adoptees' Link) in Korea, giving all my information to the president of that organization to get the ball rolling for my search. I was hesitant, feeling like I was going in uncharted waters. It was nerve-wracking, something you want to do, but you're kind of hesitant to hand personal information over. I told my parents as I went along, educated them as I was being educated. That really makes it easier when your parents can support you. You're not always having to constantly tell the reasons why you're searching and doing things, thus avoiding unnecessary fights.

G.O.A.'L said there was a newspaper that would run an ad, that supposedly reaches every Korean doorstep or almost every Korean doorstep in Seoul. The ad ended up sitting around for a few months, but eventually it did run -- a big picture of me as a kid and the information I was given concerning my background. It was January 2000 and I had already planned to go to Korea, just to kind of sightsee and start my adoption search. It was my last day on the job. I had this new job lined up, more money, more opportunities, the next step in my career. That morning when I was at work, I got this phone call from the president of G.O.A.'L. She began with some small talk and then told me that she had located my aunt and family. Utter shock and disbelief. I can't say what I said right now, but I was like, "Don't mess around with me," and she's like, "I wouldn't joke around about this," and it was kind of funny. I said, "I'll see you Tuesday." She said, "You're coming?" I said, "Yeah, I already have booked tickets."

Looking through old newspapers, my aunt had found the ad only a few days before. The ad actually only reached

62

a very small population in Seoul so it was amazing that she actually saw it. When she first glanced at the ad, I think she knew in her heart it was me, but it was such an emotional topic that she wanted to be really sure before putting my father through a roller coaster ride. She went to his house, asked for pictures of me, but didn't tell him why. It was quite a miracle when she responded to the ad. Everything she said to them was right: my Korean name, my birth date. But, then she added something I didn't know: I wasn't a foundling.

It was a chapter in my life that was waiting to be opened. I think about how this chapter wouldn't have been opened if I'd never moved to the Washington, D.C. area for college. I probably would never have gone to the "Gathering", would never have been introduced to G.O.A.'L, which suggested I run the ad. I think I knew that it was meant to happen. I think one of the main things that drove me was this feeling that something was there for me on the other side of the world. It's like I always knew that they were there waiting.

Reunion is not always a great thing. I mean it's great, but in the eyes of Koreans there has to be a separation to be a reunion. Emotions went one way, then another. To them, I was this lost child, but, at the same time, I was thinking, who are these strangers? I got over that one quickly.

When I imagined meeting my father I thought I was going to be looking in the mirror. Everyone who yearns to find his or her birth family talks about that. They think, "I really want to find someone that looks like me." We do have similar traits, but it's not like looking in the mirror, by any means. He's very thin, and I have more of the American weight on me. Actually we're the same height, or maybe he's a half-inch taller. That surprised me because everyone told me I was going to be taller than the average Korean because

63

of my American diet. Now I can tell them, "No, I'm tall not because of what I ate. It's my genetic makeup."

I discovered I am my father's only son, his eldest child. And, as the only son of a man who himself is an only son, I am the only one to carry on the family name. When we first met, my father was very, very relieved, to finally find me, very sorry for everything he had done. In a sense I accept his apology and, in a sense, I think he gave me a better opportunity. It turns out my father took care of me the first two years of my life. My mother had left, and in Korea, the father has ownership of the children. He could have let my mother take me, but he kept me and then probably thought, "How am I going to take care of this kid?" Eventually, he found out that adoption was a good thing. I think I was at an orphanage or foster home for a couple of weeks before my adoption, but my father told me he took me to the plane himself and said his goodbyes.

When I saw my siblings it was pretty surreal. I almost couldn't believe it. I have two full sisters, two half-sisters. We don't look exactly the same. With all the makeup, it was hard to see our facial commonalities, but now, when I look at pictures, I can see the resemblance. Apparently they knew they had a brother who had come to America, but as children, I think they wrote it off because I don't think anyone believed we would reunite. They didn't speak any English and thought I was real funny with the Korean words I knew, so I had a translator the whole time, which I couldn't have done without.

I gradually realized my siblings and I have similar nose and mouth structures, but it's our personality characteristics that really got me to believe that my sisters and I are the same blood. We just clicked, really clicked, right off the bat. We tend to have an understanding of one another that, to me, should take years and years to build. Maybe after only the second day of knowing my siblings, I just had that connection, that feeling of acceptance, which I can't really explain too well, but it was a good feeling.

When I saw a picture of my mother, I found my mirror. I discovered I look very much like her. That's another aspect that drives me to want to meet her. I think I inherited most of my traits from her . . . definitely in the face, we look a lot alike, and that's reassuring.

I still haven't met her. She has always been out of the family picture. I don't think my sisters really have a need to find her, have a relationship with her, but I'd like to talk to her. I don't really have any bitterness toward her, but I think my siblings do. I want to search for her, but I'm not quite sure what the best timing would be.

My second trip to Korea a year later was really solidi-fying. It convinced me that a new relationship could begin, and it helped my father and sisters realize that my coming there wasn't just a one-time event. I think they finally under-stood that I wanted to continue to visit. I told them the first time we met, but words only go so far. When I left the sec-ond time my father said he wasn't so sad because he knew he would see me again. My father has made it very easy for me to ask all the questions I want and he's very willing to give me the answers, which was a surprise to me. It's a good feeling, a closeness. He's a very caring, loving person who's raised four girls really well, and I respect him.

I'm my father's only son and I really realize how important that is. My grandmother passed away three years ago and we visited her grave, and that was a pivotal point of my first trip. From then on I really felt like his son, rather

65

than just a stranger. There are a lot of issues that I would rather not deal with right now, like who's going to take care of my father in the future and whether that's something I want to take on or not. As far as having everything that's happened complete my identity process, I think I'm fairly calm about the whole thing now, which is good in a way, but there are still things I struggle with. You're never issue-free, but then again who is? Everyone's story is unique, but there are commonalities.

Recently, I've had probably the most difficult time of my life in terms of figuring out my identity. I've been struggling with the differences in my connections with my two sets of siblings. I base most of my affection and connection with my siblings here on life experiences, growing up together and seeing one another throughout our whole lives, but I've been experiencing something very strange lately. I've been getting culture shock when I go home, back to southern Maryland, to visit my family. It's a strange feeling. I mean they're my family, and I've known them longer than I've known any family, certainly longer than I've known my family in Korea.

I've kind of embraced my Korean culture and heritage more. I'm feeling more Korean. It's not something that's forced. It's something that's come over me very naturally throughout the past few years. Going home, I can see the visual difference between me and the rest of my family a lot more now. Even our mannerisms are different. Theirs are very American, and mine are becoming more Korean, more reserved, less flamboyant. Growing up, I was more animated and now I hold back my emotions a lot more. I don't know if it's something I'm purposefully trying to do, but it's just happening. Maybe it's just the maturation process. I don't

66

know the answer, but I do know I feel much different inside my American family now, more different than ever before.

It was always obvious that I was physically different from my family, but more importantly, I always knew, deep down, that I was adopted and that was always an issue for me. Maybe my true personality traits were based more on my genetic makeup than my environment, and maybe that was a battle I always fought . . . my environment said one thing, but my genetic makeup said another. Now that I've discovered I'm a first-born child, a lot of the feelings I've experienced make sense to me. Growing up, I was the youngest in my American family, and I fought that notion every day. I hated being the youngest and always wanted to be the leader, always wanted to take charge. I hated being the one who always had to follow and wait to experience things. My mother here in the States actually mentioned recently that she always knew that I was the oldest because that's just the way I acted.

Adoption was always an issue for me, in the sense that there was always a void, a loneliness. I didn't feel complete, always thinking there was something more I had to find out. Now the void's different . . . it's been switched to my American family. I feel an emptiness because I'm Korean and they're American. I still feel a sense of belonging with them, but there's a void that's physical. It's truly amazing for me now to have such opposing feelings, depending on which family I'm with, which environment I'm in. I still haven't sorted through all the emotions yet. But I know family reunions can depress me. I feel guilty, but I realize that I really don't have anything in common with my ancestors, with my grandparents. The differences slap me in the face every day, but I know that these people are my family, the

67

only family I have ever really known. They know me better than anyone and that's a good feeling.

My sister and I didn't get along at all growing up, and that's because her personality was very much different than mine. She was very anal in a lot of ways . . . cleaned everything. Everything was perfect and she followed the rules to a T, just like a mother. Now, I think we've really grown to love one another and to appreciate one another because we understand those differences and know we can't change them. Now she understands what I was going through emotionally growing up when I threw fits and ruined her day. Before, she felt lots of resentment about having a brother who would do that. Today, those feelings have changed to thoughts of "that must've been very difficult for my brother to go through."

In high school, or early college, my sister wrote a letter describing her feelings toward me. I think she wrote it during the time when she started understanding herself better, so I really respected that, even though it wasn't something that always felt like good reading. It's interesting how, when you reach adulthood, you can kind of talk about these things on a level where you can kind of omit the emotions. It's a good feeling.

My relationship with my brother has always been pretty strong. He's always been my protector, my guiding light. He's always accepted me. I look at pictures, back in the days of growing up, and he always has his arm around me. He's always treated me like a little brother. Even now when he visits, I wake up to him pulling pranks on me. Nothing has changed. He still sees me as his brother and he always will. Racial differences were never really an issue for him. Even so, I do experience culture shock with him. I mean he likes different things and we're clearly different. He's very outdoorsy, doesn't like anything that's really commercial. He just likes basic simple things. I'm more the type of person that likes name-brand clothing, fancy cars, the nicer things in life. Maybe it's just the pop culture we grew up in, but my Korean sisters are more like me.

I'm still struggling with the fact that my brother and I have been close all our lives, but I continue to see cultural differences. There's a sub-pop culture in the Korean community that I bought into a little bit. It's hard to explain but I just know I enjoy certain things, and my brother enjoys certain things, and the way we show that is very different. His mannerisms and body language are very different than mine. He's very animated in some ways that aren't common practices in the Korean community. It's a cultural difference between Asians and Caucasians.

I think I've begun to see both sides, rather than having tunnel vision. When I grew up, I was a minority in my community, but I didn't feel like it. I never understood until I went to college, met other minorities, and became a part of the minority community. It was then that I could look back and really understand the feeling of what it was to be a minority in America. That's exactly how it's happening now. It wasn't until I found my Korean family that I finally started to get a handle on my emotions around feeling so different in the midst of my adopted family. Before, I knew there was a difference . . . now I'm understanding what those differences really entail.

I feel much more empowered as a minority now. When someone says something offensive, I feel obligated to stand up for myself, which is much different from when I was younger. Growing up, you really sink or swim and I chose

69

to swim. It's funny. People could call me any name they wanted to and it hurt, but I never had a full understanding. I never really understood prejudice and bias and racism until I started taking pride in being a minority.

I'm proud of being Asian, specifically of being Korean. Before, I think I wasn't so proud because I didn't have anything to base pride on. I was just trying to assimilate and survive. Now I have an inner sense of worth. Internally I think I'm in a great place now. I'm a lot calmer, more patient . . . that's why I call myself more stoic, more reserved. Maybe finding my birth family helped me to mature. I'm very much more at ease with myself, no longer so full of questions. The reason for my loneliness is no longer unknown. Now it's a tangible loneliness, not a feeling of what's going on, why am I feeling this way?

At times people wanted to call me a "Twinkie": white inside, yellow outside, but now people really look at me as having full knowledge and understanding of who I am. It's a very touchy issue. Some adoptees never have had the opportunity to learn about that portion of their life, and a lot of them don't even care, which is okay. I respect everyone's decision, but I think it's better to have all the facts and then make your decision. Even if I were uncomfortable with other Asians in the beginning, I still forced myself to learn about them and to make myself comfortable, because that's the only way I could develop any educated positions.

For me, there really is a lot of catching up to do. In college, the few times I went over to eat food at my Korean friends' households, I felt really happy. They'd be eating Korean food, authentic Korean food, and I'd really feel at home. People would say, "You have nothing to compare it to, so how do you feel at home?" I don't know, can't explain it. It was just something I felt very comfortable with, going from being uncomfortable to being very comfortable. The more things that helped me identify with myself, the better I felt. When I was a child it was a lose-lose situation when it came to embracing my Korean identity. There really weren't many resources, and there were no role models from my culture. People would also say, "What's the difference? Growing up is growing up." But I think it does matter. There are reasons why we have many different cultures in the world. There are different ways of doing things.

I don't think I'm the typical adoptee. I'm not trying to set myself apart, but I'm just saying that I'm an adoptee who has really embraced my culture, Korean culture, and tried to learn as much as I can. A lot of adoptees, especially ones I've met, don't really have an interest in doing that. They're kind of confident about who they are today, and that's okay. I want to say they're missing out on a lot, but maybe that's not the case. A lot of adoptees who don't feel the need to learn about their own Korean heritage, or who have a problem with other Koreans, may perhaps buy into the social stereotypes we all were raised with. Instead of really understanding what it is to be a minority, instead of embracing that, I believe they do everything to fight being placed into those stereotypes. They force themselves to assimilate even more, and when they do that, the Korean community looks at them as rejecting their heritage. I've been surprised that I do understand a lot of things that are innately Korean. Other Koreans ask me: "How do you know about that? Or why do you think that way?" I guess I have discovered that I have a lot of innate Korean traits that just come out at the funniest moments. That's why I really object when people say you're only a product of your environment.

I'm about as ambitious as they come, really strive to improve every year. I've had lots of role models from everywhere -- physicians, professors, businessmen, businesswomen. My adoptive father was probably my most significant role model. He provided for the family, had a gentle demeanor, and I realize that's the type of father every kid needs to have -- someone who can really provide for the family and be a good person and be able to manage the family in a way that's effective and not abusive. So, I think he did a very good job. I really respect both my parents for raising me well.

Since finding my birth family, I've dealt with a lot and I don't think I've given myself time to filter through it. When I was in Korea, I didn't want to show emotion at all. Not that I didn't want to, that's not the right word, but I couldn't. It was supposed to be a happy time. I didn't know when I was going to see them again. Why sit around and cry? At the same time it was hard to feel something for someone that you wanted to meet your entire life, and to have it all come out on command. That's pretty difficult.

Now I know I can hop on a plane and go see them. I know the feelings my family has toward me. They almost mirror my own toward them, so I can't ask for much more than that. I understand the reason my birthfather gave me up and I know he really regrets doing it. My father's a very sensitive man, not a typical Korean male. I feel very fortunate to have him back in my life.

Even though my adoptive parents were very happy, very supportive about my finding my birth family, I don't think it's something I can constantly have a conversation with them about. It's emotional for everyone. It's still a Catch-22 because even to this day I have to be understanding of everyone's feelings involved in this, not just my own, but also those of my parents, my siblings, my birth family. It's a lot to handle, a lot to juggle. I know adoptees have conflicting feelings, of loyalty and disloyalty, when they're looking for their birth families. But, I think my parents and I are all mature adults. These are the cards we were dealt. My parents shouldn't ever have to question whether I love them or not. Other adoptees I've spoken with sometimes say their parents play on guilt, saying things to discourage a search. They want to protect their children's feelings, but at the same time, they're protecting their own. I'm glad that this didn't happen to me.

I think it would be very interesting to see both sets of my parents in the same room, just like in the documentary "First Person Plural."[1] I think it would be more life changing for my adoptive parents than for my birthfather in Korea. My parents have seen me grow a lot over the last few years and view me in a very different light now. I hope it's because I've been open about my feelings about being adopted, bringing them into my life. They've become more educated about adoption. To them, adoption was receiving a baby, calling it their own and loving that child as their own. My perspective is much different from theirs. I think now they finally have an understanding of the differences I could never articulate as a child. I realized this during the showing of "First Person Plural" that we attended. My dad was emotional . . . I've never seen him react so strongly to something so personal to me, and that was a good feeling . . . made me feel like

[1] "First Person Plural" by Korean-born filmmaker Deann Borshay Liem depicts her efforts to reconcile her life as an adoptee in the United States with her unknown beginnings in Korea. It premiered as part of the PBS series P.O.V. in December 2000.

he really loved me. It was great to have a film express and communicate so much of what I've been feeling since childhood.

My first reaction is to say I was never bitter about being adopted, but I'm sure there were points in my childhood when I was. Yet, to this day, I'm not someone that says, "Why did you do it?" I have accepted it, and so I never had to really press that issue. To be honest, it's something that's kind of unspoken, and maybe that's because I'm happy with my life now. Maybe if I were really unhappy, I would be angrier. But, I will say I am kind of bitter that I didn't have the chance to be raised with my siblings, with my four sisters in Korea. I miss them a lot. We stay in contact. I call them; they call me. In fact, we talk every week. They've learned a little English and I speak a little Korean.

At this point, I feel like I'm a Korean caught in an American world, very Korean American now. I'm sure Korean Americans who aren't adopted have the same exact feelings. Some emotions thought to be unique to adoption really aren't. I think that's maybe another reason there needs to be more discussions among all Korean Americans. I'm still struggling with the fact that I have two families: one in Korea, one here, pretty far away from each other. I do feel like I want to spend some part of my life in Korea, but I don't know how . . . my life is here . . . I think that's going to be an ongoing struggle for a while.

Todd Knowlton, 33
Consultant
North Bethesda, Maryland

74

PHOTO GALLERY

Todd Knowlton

Jesse Nickelson

Ami Nafzger

PHOTO GALLERY

Kathleen Bergquist

Frances Gipson

Adam Carlson

Becca

People who know about my adoption have told me I should write a book. I always laugh at them and say, "Who would want to read it?" But, if I ever did write one, it would start out like this. I was born February 23, 1961. This is what is on my documentation, but who knows if it is true. I'm not clear how long I lived at the Dong Sung Won Orphanage in Pusan. The paperwork I have, that my father meticulously kept, starts when I was transferred to Holt orphanage in Seoul on March 7, 1962.

My dad, Thomas Higgins, was a Methodist minister and my mom, Nancy, was a teacher, soon to be a stay-at-home mom. My parents adopted me because they had been trying to get pregnant and it wasn't happening. They had basically been told that their

75

chances of having children were slim to none. My father was in the seminary at the time and he was having a problem with a class and happened to meet with a teacher who had adopted a son from Korea. When my dad came home, he talked to my mom about it and that's what set the seed for my adoption.

According to the Korean government, I was legally adopted in 1963 but my parents couldn't get me into the States for another whole year because of red tape. I ended up spending two years in the orphanage because they couldn't get my visa from the U. S. government. My dad wrote letters to our local congressman trying to get some of the paperwork moving.

By the time I finally arrived in the States, it was March 20, 1964. I was 3 years old and my mother was six months pregnant with my sister, Debby. My first home was Lower Berkshire Valley, New Jersey. I am the oldest of three children and the only adopted one. My parents divorced when I was about 9 years old, my sister was 6 and my brother, Tom, was 3. My dad later remarried and had two more children, Joanna and Susie. So I guess, technically, I'm one of five.

I was raised as a Caucasian. By that I mean that when we talked about family things, we always talked about my mother's and my father's families, so my being Korean was never introduced into the picture. I was raised as if I belonged to the family and that their family history was my history. My mother's background was German-English and I think my father is Irish. My mom said the social worker had told them to Americanize me, that it would confuse me to know anything about the Korean culture.

For a short time when I was about 5 years old, my dad knew some Korean people, but back then I didn't want to learn any Korean. I guess I was just getting comfortable with English. I regret not taking an interest because it was to be my only chance at learning about my heritage for a very long time. I tried to learn about Korea when I was in middle and high school, but the only books I found were on the war and travel guides.

It was probably in first grade when it became really noticeable that I was different. At that point children started making fun of how I looked. We had moved to a new town, Belvidere, New Jersey, where I would grow up, and it was very rural, lots of farms, and sort of redneck, a backwards sort of area. The town was so small, only about a mile wide. There wasn't much to do within the town itself: no movie theaters, no mall, no pizza parlors, nothing to do other than in the summer when you went to the pool.

Kids made fun of me by calling me "chink" and by singing that little ditty that children say about the Chinese . . . about the "slanty-eyed" something. I would come home in tears and my mom would just say, "It's okay. They don't know what they're talking about." She never really addressed why the children were calling me this. My parents never really discussed those issues. My mom just sort of ignored it all and my father, he's just very introverted, and doesn't really talk a lot about stuff, and when I was old enough to really talk to him about it, I didn't see him that often, maybe every other weekend. It wasn't conducive to talking about anything in any depth. The only thing my parents would ever say about the adoption was that your parents loved you enough that they couldn't take care of you, that they gave you a chance at a better life.

It was hard being the only minority growing up. I would get questions about where I was from. Most adoptees know the scenario. "Where are you from? No, where are you really from?" People always told me I spoke good English and asked where I learned it. I became very flippant and I'd answer the language question by saying "the same place you did." They would get this puzzled look. I would then say "SCHOOL!"

When my parents divorced it was very traumatic. There was a very big sense of loss. I blamed myself for what happened. My mother said it was because they couldn't get along, but deep down in my heart I thought it was because they adopted me. That was my thinking, as a child, not understanding what was going on, except knowing that they were constantly arguing. I felt that somehow it was linked to me because I was the oldest and if I had been better, or smarter, or something, that they would have stayed together. I've talked with other kids of divorce and they've all felt the same way, that somehow it was their fault, even though it really wasn't. It is a very common feeling, but in my case, I attributed it to my being adopted.

The situation became such a battleground because my parents were still in the same town and my father was the minister and his wife, the minister's wife, had left him. They fought viciously over who would have custody. My sister and brother were young enough not to remember the fighting. I can remember being taken into the judge's chamber and being really afraid because I thought I was in trouble. He asked me which parent I wanted to live with and I remember thinking to myself that I wanted to live with my dad. I was torn because I knew the answer that was expected of me would be to stay with my mom. If I said my dad, I knew that I would be separated from my sister and brother, so I told the judge I wanted to stay with my mother. It was hard giving that answer because I truly felt my dad loved me more. As I grew up, that perception would change because of my mom's hate towards my dad.

Shortly after the divorce my dad kidnapped us for a week because my mom wouldn't let him take us on vacation. She says it was because it was just before school was starting. I can remember being in a lot of pain because my ear was infected, but my dad couldn't risk going to a doctor to get more medicine. He let me talk to my mother quickly just so she would know we were okay. It was the last contact I had until we were brought home. He knew that my mom had probably called the police. It was so traumatic that I've blocked that time period out of my memory. The only things I remember are eating tons of hotdogs and peanut butter and jelly sandwiches.

My parents fought viciously over the years. It was very hard being the pawn in the power struggles. But my dad always made me feel like he wanted and loved me. He shows my picture to anyone who looks Korean and I know he would have made the effort to keep my heritage. He always came to any activity I let him know about. I just wish I could have appreciated it more. I am fortunate that he married a wonderful woman named Janice who loves my siblings and me without any reservation. I always knew that I could talk with her and she would listen. I felt like I would have had an easier time with them, but I let the hate my mother felt towards him color my feelings. I guess I was afraid of having that hate turned to me. The 3-year-old child inside was scared of being abandoned again so I chose to stay with my mom. Many times I wonder what might have happened if I had gone to live with them.

When I was in middle school, I tried to learn something

79

about Korea because I wanted to know where I came from. Yes, it was like, I know I'm Korean, but I know nothing about the culture, nothing about my heritage, and so I went looking, trying to find something to explain why the kids picked on me, or something to arm myself with to use against the children who were harassing me. But, at that time, there just wasn't anything there.

When I did show interest in Korea, my mom told me about the social worker's advice to Americanize me as soon as possible. She didn't feel it was important for me to learn about my culture. I think she had problems with me being Korean after she divorced my dad. I always felt that she had a problem explaining me. International adoption wasn't prevalent then and people always asked her if I was from a previous marriage. She liked to tell people that I was "the milkman's." What a wonderful legacy to grow up with! It made me feel like she didn't want me. Most people assumed that she had remarried and had more children because they looked like her. I was the only one who didn't fit into the picture. I was the square peg.

It didn't help that my mother obviously favored my sister, Debby, when we were growing up. She was the really smart one, always was the perfect child, and she tended to be the squealer, the tattler about things. Whenever that happened, I'm the one that got beaten. My mother never hit Deb or Tom as much or with as much violence as she hit me. It was hard growing up not knowing if the treatment I received was because I was the oldest, Korean, adopted, or all of the above. When my mother got mad, she would lose it and just beat me, even break hairbrushes over me. It didn't happen a lot, but when it did, it was brutal and when my sister said something as an adult to her, my mother claimed that she

80

never did that. My mother wrote me a letter basically saying that she spanked all of the children and that I was the oldest, so more was expected of me. She didn't really apologize, just basically made excuses for it. My mom's reality and mine are so different.

I get along with my sister really well now as an adult, but as a child, I did not like her, and she knows that I didn't. We've discussed it and she never realized that kind of animosity was there because I kept a lot of it inside. I knew that if I didn't, it would just cause more problems. I kept diaries because that was the only way I could deal with it. Deb was very shocked at how I felt and said she thought we got along fine. I said, "Yeah, well, just don't read my diaries."

My relationship with my mom has improved over the years. I understand a little bit more about what made her do some of the things she did. But at times it seems like the past was just yesterday. It hit home when my sister received her doctorate. My mom had retired and moved to Massachusetts to live next to my sister. The graduation party was at Deb's house and most of the people invited knew both my mom and Deb. One of Deb's friends introduced herself and told me that I looked like my mom. I laughed, pointed to my mom, and said, "Yeah, we have black hair and brown eyes." She looked at me puzzled. I asked her who she thought was my mom. She pointed to Janice, my stepmother, who is sometimes asked if she is part Asian because of her almond-shaped eyes. The woman then said she didn't know that my mom had another daughter and asked me my name. She said that of course she knew Deb and had heard about my brother. I was a total surprise to her. This wasn't the first time an incident like this had happened. I found out that it still had

81

the power to hurt even after all these years . . . I've resigned myself to saying "whatever."

I was not a model student. I B'd and C'd through a lot of stuff, so I threw that stereotype right out the window. School was hard for me. I mean math was the bane of my existence. I didn't pass a math class and my mother wasn't any help. She's not good at math either, but she didn't try to get me any help even though I was flunking.

In high school I found a small group of friends. They were from another town and hadn't heard the stories about my family. I didn't have many friends before then and at the time I didn't understand if it was just because I was adopted, if it was because I was Asian, or if it was because my parents had such a nasty divorce . . . the town got dragged into it because my father preached from the pulpit and then my mom left the church and went to another church and the minister testified against her in divorce court.

Making friends was difficult because my father had moved and was very religious about taking us every other weekend and three weeks out of the summer. When you're being shuttled off to another town every other weekend, you really couldn't form friendships in either place because you weren't around at the time when kids would do things together.

The few friends that I did have were Caucasians. I always thought of myself as white. It was when I looked into the mirror or saw the looks on people's faces when I was with my family that I remembered I wasn't. I was the only minority student until my freshman year in high school when I saw an African-American senior. Parents wouldn't let their children out with him, even in a group setting. He asked my mom's friend's daughter to the prom, but she refused to let

82

her daughter go. He had to go to other schools to get dates. I guess I was lucky that way since people didn't mind me going out in groups with their kids. They just didn't want me to date their sons.

In my sophomore year there was another Asian girl that entered the school. A few months later her parents transferred her to a private school because the students harassed her so badly. I can remember being jealous that her parents loved her enough to transfer her. When I had troubles with kids teasing me, my mom's answer was, "Just ignore them."

It's hard when they follow you home, taunting you all the way. You know that if you reacted it would just make it worse. I got very good at blocking things out, locking everything inside. I didn't have anyone to turn to for help. It was enough of a scandal that the minister's wife left him. You can't keep secrets in small towns. Depression and suicidal thoughts were my constant companions.

By the time I was a junior the harassment at school was getting really bad and I was getting picked on a lot. I'd have people stealing my books, kids putting gum on the back of my shirt, little side comments about "chinks," and guys coming up and saying, "Oh, do you do it differently?" I was like, "Go away," but guys would make rude comments to my boyfriend like, "Oh, you must be having a hot time with her."

Really, honestly, my mother just sort of never helped me with any of these problems. If it didn't pertain to her directly, she couldn't be bothered, pretty much, and you learn very quickly not to go looking for help because you know you're not going to get any. When I finally did say to my mom that I'm really having a lot of issues and I'm very suicidal and I'd like to go see a doctor, she basically said, "It's a stage you're going through and everybody goes through it."

83

And, when I asked if I could go live with my father because the school district he was in was a little more racially diverse and I wouldn't be the only minority, she had a conniption, screaming and yelling, and putting my father down.

My suicidal thoughts continued, but I was a chicken, like if I could have gotten pills, I probably would have taken them. I would wish I were dead, you know, thoughts like: Nobody would care if I weren't here, nobody would miss me. Or, why am I here? Why am I suffering like this? I would often wonder if the breakup of my parents was because of me.

It wasn't until I was a senior in high school that I realized that it wasn't my fault. We had to do a report in health class and we had to write a term paper about anything that you wanted to write about, and my paper was on children of divorce. I wanted to see what was out there. I used a book that was written in 1964, and my teacher asked if it was still relevant, and I said, "Oh my God, when I read the book I saw me through the whole thing." Everything they talked about, the feelings of guilt, that if you had done something better, your parents would still be together . . . it was all there. I also realized at that point that it wasn't me that caused the divorce and that helped me deal with it a little better.

Despite all this I did date two guys in high school. The first was from an Italian family. His mother was Italian and she really didn't like me because I was not Italian, and not Catholic. The father loved me and I really had a good relationship with him. That was like my freshman year and I dated him for maybe eight months. I think I was surprised when somebody showed any interest in me because I had just thought of myself as being the oddball and that nobody really liked me. There used to be a bike shop in town, and he was really into biking, and it was on my way home, so

84

he'd be hanging out at the bike shop, and I'd drop in because I knew the owners. That was sort of my hangout place. We broke up because he was only interested in sex.

I started dating my next boyfriend, Mike, probably at the end of sophomore year, and then we dated all the way through high school. We were in the band together, spent a lot of time together and I knew his sisters who were in the grades above. We had talked about getting married. I was going to go to college and he was going into the Air Force, and so we sort of put everything on hold.

His father hated me. I don't think my being adopted affected that as much as the fact that I was Korean, specifically Korean, because supposedly when his father found out that Mike was dating me, he said that I had killed his best friend in the Korean War. He didn't say that directly to me, but it came out later that he had said that to Mike.

For me, not having been born until 1961, it was like, "Okay . . . how do the numbers work on that one?" Actually, it was odd growing up at that time because I was alive after the Korean War, during the Vietnam War, and people who saw me tended, if they had any bias against Asians, to blame me for every Asian war. It was like, "Okay, I wasn't old enough for Korea, and I'm not Vietnamese." But people would tend to lump me with anything that they had negatives against, with either one of those wars or with what their friends or their fathers had brought back from those wars about fast women. Mike's father told him that he didn't want slant-eyed grandchildren and didn't like "niggers", "chinks" or "whores." His mentality pretty much summed up the area.

A month or so before I left for college my mother sort of came out of the closet and had her partner, Kathy, move in with her. Deb and Tom were the ones who got the bulk

85

of being raised in a gay relationship . . . they were the ones who had to live in a small town with a mother who was now openly gay. I really didn't ever have a relationship with my brother because he was six years younger and we were always at different stages of development. But, even to this day, he has no relationship with any of us. He doesn't talk to my mother, my father, my sister or me. I think, in his case, a lot of it had to do with my mother coming out. I didn't really have to deal with any of it too much and even though my mom and Kathy have been together over 25 years, my mother has never discussed it. That's pretty much how my mom deals with everything.

I dropped out of college in February 1980, during my first year. I just had an emotional breakdown, couldn't handle being there, so I left. I was at Wilson College in Chambersburg, Pennsylvania. I became seriously depressed and I couldn't handle the workload and I just was very cut off and isolated. It was a small girls' school, so there weren't that many people around and I was from a small town and it was my first time away from home, so I had a hard time coping. I didn't have any support from home either. Nobody ever called me to see how I was doing or wrote letters, or checked in on me. I didn't know what to do about it. I'd always kept everything in, so for me to go out and ask for help was a foreign idea.

At one point, the college was renting out part of the school to some business, and there were guys there, and I became friends with one of them who was going through a rough time. He and I had thought about chucking it all and taking off together. That was how bad it was . . . he was like, "You give me the go, and we're out of here."

When I told my mother that I was having problems, that

I was really depressed, she said, "I think you should stick it out until the end of the semester. There's no reason for you to come home." I said, "Okay, fine, but when you come at the end of the semester, there's no guarantee what shape I'm going to be in because I am about ready to like, lose it. I am so close to the edge . . . there's no guarantee what you'll find when you finally pick me up at the end of the year." I guess something registered and she came and picked me up.

I went back home to New Jersey to live with my mom and Kathy. My mom got me a part-time job with her school system, so I was helping out as a teacher's aide with the learning-disabled children in the school where she taught. Then I ended up working full time for about a year and a half with seriously disabled children at Hunterdon State School.

I met my husband Kerry at Kathy's 30th birthday party. His stepfather was Kathy's boss and so they invited his whole family. According to him, he and I used to run cross-country and he wanted to get to know me but he was too shy to actually come up and do anything about it. His mother persuaded him to come to the party and we just sort of hit it off. After all my negative dating experiences I knew I wanted to be involved with someone who accepted me, who wasn't going to ask if I did it differently than white girls. Kerry was the first man I dated who didn't care what color I was, who didn't have any preconceived ideas of what I was supposed to be like from stories told about the war. His parents didn't care what I looked like and just accepted me for who I was. Their family already was international and I think that's why I really liked them. They accepted me. His older brother had married a girl from the Philippines and his oldest sister's husband was from Puerto Rico. It didn't bother them to have a Korean adoptee added to the family. It's ironic that my first

87

Asian friends would be introduced to me through Kerry. He fenced and there were a lot of Asians in the fencing world.

I dated him for six months before we got engaged, and then we ended up waiting about a year before we got married. That was in 1981. We were just trying to get ourselves on our feet, and we had a lot of battles with my mother over wedding plans. She did not approve of us getting married, said I was too young, needed to finish college, etc. My father just wanted whatever made me happy, but he really didn't have much say . . . he was the only one who wasn't really giving objections. My mother was giving enough for both.

So, we contacted everybody about three weeks before the wedding and cancelled the big ceremony. We had a very small wedding, called people up three hours before and said, "If you can be here, nice, if you can't, fine."

My mother had been giving me such a hassle over it. She didn't want to pay for the wedding, didn't want to go into hock. I mean, this was the story of my life. If I wanted anything, I had to earn the money for it. If I wanted to go to college, get a car, clothing beyond what was normal, I had to work for it. I started working when I was in fifth grade because I wanted to go to college.

My sister, Deb, said that she got the same sort of spiel, but I don't know how much being adopted makes you take it more to heart when things are being said because you always have that deep down fear that you're going to be rejected. Maybe it's because I was 3 when I was adopted, so I know there are memories locked inside my head. I can always remember feeling that if I didn't behave, or if I didn't do what my mom said, that she'd send me back. I do remember her telling me when I wouldn't eat stuff, "Well, think of all the starving children in Korea." I can remember getting slapped

88

because I said, "Well, let's box it up and send it to them."

In 1999 I went to the first international "Gathering" of Korean adoptees and one of them, who was adopted when she was 9 months old, was complaining about everybody always telling her she should be grateful about being adopted. One of the women at the table said, "Well, I wasn't adopted until I was like 8 or 9, and I'll tell you what you should be grateful for," proceeding to tell her what she went through growing up in the orphanage. I relayed that to my mother, and my mother was like, "Oh yeah, you hid food when you came over."

I really did react when I heard that because I had to mourn for the 3-year-old girl I had been. She had to know to hide food because she didn't know when she was going to get the next meal. So I think, growing up, a lot of that did play into how I dealt with things on a subconscious level.

I knew I had been in an orphanage before I was adopted, but the only thing I know about my birth family is just what my parents told me at the time, which was that my parents loved me enough to give me a better chance at life. That's all they ever said about it and I don't remember asking many questions about my adoption. It was just sort of one of those things that I guess I asked and it just sort of got sloughed off. After awhile you stop asking. I knew that I had birthparents, family . . . somewhere.

My father said that when they decided to adopt me they were sent pictures of children and then you were supposed to send back the pictures of the children you didn't want. I have a copy of the picture of me and my father has the original. He carries it in his wallet. It's pretty battered now. He pulls it out and shows anyone he thinks is Korean, or people with adopted children. He goes up and says, "Hi, my oldest daughter is adopted from Korea," and shows them the picture. It wasn't until I was a teenager that I was aware he was doing this. At the time I was embarrassed, but as an adult, it's like pretty neat because he's proud of me.

I'd always had thoughts about searching, but it wasn't one of those things that you did easily . . . we didn't have the Internet, traveling that far was a luxury, people just didn't fly to Korea on a whim. Now people go over there and teach English as a second language, and there are opportunities for Korean adoptees to go back, do birth searches, explore their heritage, get jobs. But, 20 years ago, it wasn't really something you could do without a lot of money or connections.

For me that first "Gathering" in 1999 was a life-altering event, making me much more comfortable with myself as a Korean adoptee. For the first time I saw people that looked like me, talked like me, and had the same issues. Talking to people was amazing because you're sitting there thinking that I was going through all of this in my life believing I was doing it alone, and here were all these people, and we were doing the same thing, all thinking that we were the only ones, and we weren't. I made some really good friendships there that I still have to this day. We have mini-Gatherings every six months, and with the Internet, my communications with people have just opened up in an amazing way. Before the "Gathering" I didn't even have the idea that it would be possible to try searching for my birth family. The friends I met there gave me the support and the courage to search.

Back in 1991 when the Koreans opened up their records I wrote to Holt in Eugene, Oregon to get a copy of my records and that's how I discovered that I wasn't from Seoul, which was what everybody had been told and which was on my birth certificate. But on the Holt paperwork, it said that I was

90

from Pusan. It was sort of shocking to find out that here I was, thinking I was from Seoul, when I was from half way across the country. I had hoped that Holt would have even more information than that, but there was nothing else that I didn't already know.

In 2000 I decided to search through Global Oversees Adoptees' Link (G.O.A'L) I sent them what I knew: my case number, the name that I had, that I had scarring on my body and that, according to the paperwork, I was born Feb. 23, 1961. I got one response and they thought that I was their younger sister that had been given up. It got to the point where they had us do a DNA test. But, I felt like it would be too easy that the first family that answered the ad would be mine. It seemed too bizarre, not possible, but I know deep down inside I was hoping it was a match. I was very disappointed when the testing came back negative. If I had been the sister that they thought I was, I would have been a twin, with a brother that had also been given up for adoption. That sort of really threw me for a loop.

It was about a week before our mini-Gathering in Los Angeles that I found out about the negative results. Everybody knew that I was searching, cause I was talking in e-mails about my search and people were asking how it was going. It was like a whole community came together and said, "Gee, we're really sorry . . . things will work out . . . you know we're there for you." I have discovered that the people I met at the "Gathering" and the mini-Gatherings are my Korean family. Every time I go to one it's like finding more family. It doesn't matter how long between the events, everyone picks up like it was yesterday. It's like a big family reunion. I guess it really is.

I went through a mourning period for what could have

91

been. I had to remind myself that my husband, Kerry, my children and my friends loved me and it wasn't the end of the world. Ironically, when I told my mom I was doing a birth search, that was probably the only time that she showed any support toward me. I think it's something she could relate to since her mother died during childbirth.

I have two children, a daughter named Kyra, born in 1991, and a son named Justin, born in 1994. It was incredible when I had my own children, to finally look at somebody else and say, "Oh my God, here's somebody that looks like me . . . this is my family." I can see my eyes, I can see that they have my smile, but they certainly don't have my eyelashes. It was a great feeling because suddenly there was somebody that looked like you and that you could love.

Kerry and I have talked about the adoption with our kids. I don't hide it. They've heard me talking to people because I've had Koreans come up to me while my kids are there and say, "Why don't you speak Korean?" I say, "Well, because I'm adopted and my parents are white." It's not unusual for us to see Koreans because in the area where we live there's a large Korean population as well as every other nationality. When my children's elementary school had international day, there were 80 countries represented.

If I had grown up in this kind of atmosphere I think I would have had a little easier time dealing with stuff because if there were more people that looked like me, I wouldn't have felt the harassment so deeply. I might have come to an understanding that it was against the nationality, not taking it as a personal attack. Where I grew up, anything that was directed at me was a personal attack, because there weren't any other minorities. When my husband and I discussed having children, where to settle became a major issue. I could

92

not raise our children in a town that was not racially diverse. I did not want my children going through what I had gone through growing up. We are fortunate to have settled in a diverse area in Maryland, just outside Washington, D.C. My children have not encountered the hate or prejudices that I experienced. Their schools look like the League of Nations.

In 2003, I went back to Korea for the first time since my adoption. Before my trip I had decided not to do any more searching for my birth family while I was there. I pretty much thought that it was a dead end. I was going on 43 years old, and depending on how old my parents were at the time, they might not be alive. Was I the oldest, the youngest or the middle child? I didn't really think anybody was alive that would remember even if I had any information to go on. Basically what I wanted to do was close the circle. I had gone to Oregon and I had seen my records there and I wanted to go to Holt in Seoul and to Pusan, to the orphanage, to just look at the records. I didn't expect to find anything new, but I just wanted to physically touch the beginning of my life, as I know it, just physically tic up loose ends, saying, "Okay, I've done everything I can do to search for family, and this is it."

I can't explain the incredible feelings that overwhelmed me as the day of trip got closer. I was going back to a country I didn't remember with all the fear, excitement and wonder of returning 40 years after I left. It would be a place where people would look like me, but where I could not speak the same language.

I think my first impression was how very quiet the plane was. No one spoke loudly and the plane smelled different. It had a very twilight-zone feeling. No one was speaking English. The sound of Korean pulled at me and I kept thinking

93

that if I listened hard enough it would make sense.

I was very glad to be going with two close friends, also Korean adoptees, one I met at the first "Gathering" in 1999 and the other, Mindy, I knew from a mini-Gathering in California. I joked around that I was an East Coast girl going back East. I had warned them when the trip was in the planning stages that I might have panic attacks or flashbacks because I wasn't sure if going back to Korea would trigger anything. Unlike me, they both were adopted in infancy so flashbacks are something they've never experienced.

Our first experience on landing at Incheon airport was the language barrier. We really were strangers in a strange land, navigating through customs and exchanging money, not knowing how to communicate with anyone. We had to find a bus that would take us to the hotel nearest where we were staying, and then when we arrived there we tried to get a taxi to drive us to the youth hostel, KoRoot, that had just opened up that summer. The taxi driver didn't understand us but fortunately we had a phone number, and the person there was able to tell the taxi driver in Korean where it was. We arrived and then had to walk down an alley, tired, scared and unsure that we were heading in the right direction. Finally we found the hostel and the other adoptees there and the management helped, getting us familiar with everything.

The next day was filled with going to Holt's post-adoption services. I didn't know what to expect. It would be the only time we would not have a translator with us. I can speak a little Korean. I had learned some of it from tapes and I tried to remember phrases I'd heard. I had taken Korean classes at the college where I work. I joked around with my friends that I knew dog Korean, "sit, stay, come, stop barking, house." I was relieved to see that the subway

94

maps were familiar in their layout. At least I could read the Korean alphabet, so I knew where we had to transfer trains or get off.

Mindy and I looked through our files. I was disappointed when I saw that mine only had three pages and the first two were the same as the file in Eugene. The third was a medical profile. When I said, "Is this all there is?" the social worker told me that the files were in Oregon. I knew that I wasn't going to get anywhere, that there was no hope of finding new information. It hit home that my birth search had officially ended. The 3-year-old inside me cried and wondered if anyone even cared what had happened to her. But, I just had to deal with it, you know, because I really never expected to find anything.

The second day a friend came to act as translator and tour guide. He helped us navigate shopping for hanboks . . . just amazing. I wanted to stop and see all the fabric and dresses. It wasn't anything like shopping in the United States. He tried to show us the fine art of bargaining, something we weren't used to. Our next stop was Dongdaemun & Namdaemun markets. The sights and sounds seemed strange, yet so familiar. I kept asking what this was or that was in Korean . . . I felt like a little kid with 1000 questions out shopping for the first time. My friend laughed because he said I sounded like a kyopo (overseas Korean) when I asked how much something cost. If I wanted to sound more like a native, I needed to ask "olma aeyo?"

We met our other translator who helped us get the train to Pusan, now called Busan, where she had grown up. She was wonderful and very helpful when we toured Dong Sung Won Orphanage . . . it's where my paperwork starts. The director showed me the earliest record book that they had, but it was four years after I was there. Lots of the records were lost to flooding. The orphanage had been moved three times since I was there in 1962.

Emotionally it was very hard to look at the record book and know that I had been in a book like one of those. I was glad I had tissues. The good thing was getting the tour of the facilities. We met some of the people who took care of the children who seemed very happy. I was glad to hear that they were going to school and learning about their culture and language.

We were in awe when we visited the magnificent temples -- breathtaking views and so calm and peaceful. I understood why the monks would want to live there. I found myself talking in a hushed voice.

The two most sobering points in our visit were the trips to the DMZ and to the Korean War memorial. I started to understand the great sacrifices that were made to make South Korea free. We had to bring our passports with us to show the guards that we were citizens of another country. I was disheartened to find out that at that time South Koreans weren't allowed to visit the DMZ.

There were many times during this trip that I tried to find the answers to the phantom smells and tastes that have come to me over the years. I kept hoping that I'd find something that would let me know that these were the things I remember smelling and tasting as a little girl, something that would jog my memories. I loved wandering through all the market places, the sights and smells . . . having tea in the tea houses, wishing we had places like that in the States. I guess our version is Starbucks.

I was sad to see how much the West has invaded Korea . . . everywhere you turned in Seoul you saw an American

96

franchise. Busan was more like what I had envisioned as Korea, beautiful countryside, spectacular sunrises over the harbor. Busan seemed more traditional than Seoul. My analogy was: Seoul was like Los Angeles and Busan was like San Francisco.

I felt like, in some sense, I had come home. I looked like everyone else. It was the first time that I felt like I belonged. No one looked at me like I was a foreigner. It was strange to have people come up in the subway and ask me directions, even if I did only recognize the word for "where." I realized I was comfortable with myself and where I was. My friends had many laughs over my attempts at speaking Korean, but I looked at it as an adventure. I still hesitate to speak Korean with native speakers here at home but for some reason I didn't feel as awkward speaking Korean in Korea.

The trip taught me a lot about myself. I'm more comfortable now going into the Korean markets and restaurants around where I live. There are times I feel a kind of homesickness, but I think it's more of a cultural sadness. I know that for three years I was a Korean child, living a Korean life. Korea is like a long lost friend. I wish I knew more about Korea, but I'm learning and I'm passing it all on to my children. It's a wonderful thing . . . we're all learning about our heritage at the same time. I know that I'll go back someday with my family.

How would I describe myself now?

I am a Strong-Willed Asian Woman, a S.W.A.W. in all my glory. An adoptee's husband coined the phrase at the first "Gathering" and the other husbands all laughed. It is so true. Most of us do not fit the classic stereotype of an Asian woman. We can be very outspoken and aren't going to be found walking 10 steps behind anyone. We blow the

97

stereotypes right out of the water.

People ask Kerry if he's intimidated by my exploring my heritage. He likes to answer that he married a Korean who is becoming more Korean. He thinks it's great that I'm finding a new comfort level with being a Korean adoptee.

I am a constantly evolving Korean-American adoptee.

Becca Higgins Swick, 46
Data Entry Assistant
Howard Community College
Columbia, Maryland

A.J.

All I know is what my mother told me: I was left on the steps of an orphanage. That's not much to go on. As a Korean-American adoptee, finding my identity has been a long and arduous journey, and one that is not soon to be over. This trek through unknown territory has brought me pain, laughter, anger, love, hate, despair, triumph, loneliness and joy. It has served to make me who I am.

I was 4 months old when I was adopted by my Italian mother and Danish father in 1973. Three years later they adopted my younger sister, also from Korea. My parents never spoke much about Korea or about my sister and me being Korean. I think that had to do with two things. First, my family does not know much about Korean culture or history. Second, I think my mother and father never saw us as different from themselves or others in our community. I think they thought if they loved us enough, other people wouldn't see the difference either.

However, my mother did say she took my sister and me to social gatherings with other adoptees from the Holt agency and their families. I have seen pictures from these events, but I was so young that I don't have any memories of being there. For a while, my mother did keep in contact with another woman who had two little girls from Korea, but this woman had a lot of emotional problems and they really lost touch.

Today, my mother tells me how guilty she feels for not involving us more in our Korean culture. I am sure other parents may feel this way, but I also believe that my parents did the best they could at that particular time. I did not blame my mother then for not exposing me more to my culture, nor do I now, for she loves my sister and me more than I could ever hope for a parent to love a child.

When I was 3 and my sister just a few months old, my parents divorced. My mother raised us with the help of my maternal grandparents. Money was tight and we had our difficult times, but my mother worked so hard to try to give us the best of things. Again, she wanted us to be like all the other children our age. She is a saint in my view, but no matter how hard she tried or loved us, we would, in one way or another, be different from our peers.

We grew up Catholic in a very conservative and ethnically homogeneous community in Grand Rapids, Michigan. It was difficult growing up in a city with very few Asians or other people of color, never feeling that I could identify with anyone . . . never seeing anyone who looked

100

like me in books, magazines, on television or in sports.

Around the age of 5, I remember having a vague feeling that I wasn't like the other kids. At 6, this indescribable feeling became somewhat more concrete. For instance, a Caucasian girl in my neighborhood -- someone I rode bikes with a few times -- asked me if I could see like she could. Since my eyes were not as big and round as hers, she must have wondered if I viewed the world from a panoramic perspective. Around this age and throughout grade school, many children and teenagers would look at me and then use their index fingers to tug at the outside corners of their eyes, while mimicking an Asian-sounding language. As they burst into laughter, I would pretend to ignore this teasing and mockery, even though I was filled with rage.

Having a sister from Korea didn't help my feeling of being alone, being different. I was young, more self-centered, and didn't think much about our being from the same country. When we were growing up, we would fight like sisters would, but then we'd play together and love each other. So, I never really thought much about her being adopted, about us being adopted, or not being biologically related. I never saw her as a reflection of who I was except for once, in grade school, when she was beaten up. That is when I felt that connection.

She was in third or fourth grade and a boy punched her in the stomach, had her on the ground, and kept kicking her. She was badly hurt. Because we were both so young at the time I can't really say if she was beaten up because she was Korean. But, because I also got picked on, I was thinking, oh, this could happen to me.

Throughout my life I have been called names like "chink," "Jap," "Yoko Ono" and "Twinkie" (white on the

101

inside and yellow on the outside). When I was younger I never did anything about it nor did anyone else. In seventh grade a nun who taught music called me "China girl" in front of the entire class. Not wanting to attract more attention, I just sat with my head bowed down, never making eye contact with her. In high school other girls called me "Suzy Wan" and "Short Round" (from the Indiana Jones movie). Again, I never said anything.

My Catholic high school reflected the almost exclusively Caucasian population of my community. The most I learned about my Korean culture was what I was taught in school. I was ashamed and embarrassed to sit through history class, where I learned about the evil and uncivilized "Orientals." After all, at my school, and in my community, all Asians were viewed as the same. It was just that the Eurocentric books we used made me feel shameful of my cultural heritage. The black and white text would stare at me, telling me how other countries were being "saved" from communism, hedonism, disease and starvation by the mighty, powerful and infallible United States. There wasn't an appreciation for other perspectives, and the Germans, the Japanese and the Koreans were always seen as the enemy, the bad people. I associated that viewpoint with meaning I'm not good.

In fact, during high school I never identified myself as Korean because I thought it symbolized something dirty and foreign. Instead, I claimed the heritage of my parents; in part, I think, to prevent answering questions about my Korean culture -- I felt embarrassed because it was something I knew nothing about. But, when I would say I was Italian/ Danish, people always looked at me with a puzzled face. Then I would say I was adopted and they would respond with, "Oh."

I recall many nights where I prayed and prayed that I could just be like all of the other kids. I longed for bouncy blond curls and sparkling blue eyes with a crease in my lid so I knew where to put my eye shadow when I played dress up. I later realized I would never look like the All-American Chrissy from "Three's Company" or one of the "Charlie's Angels." I was the kid who was always picked last for somebody's team during gym class and recess. Even though I had close girlfriends, I felt ugly, strange and unpopular. I didn't even bother talking to them about how I felt because I figured they're white and they're not going to get it.

For 10 years I studied tap, jazz and ballet. Dance made me feel as though I belonged. Even though not all the other students were accepting, my instructors never treated me differently. When the music played and my muscles stretched and my heart began to beat faster, I felt free, alive and powerful -- and in control. I could forget about all the things that hurt me, but I guess they were never far from my mind. Whenever we performed "The Nutcracker," I remember making sure I wasn't typecast in the role of the Chinese dancer. I guess some of the parents thought it would be appropriate for me to play that part, but I deliberately messed up when we would audition.

I never spoke up or told anyone how I felt growing up as a Korean adoptee because I didn't feel like anybody, even my family, would understand. How could they when they'd never gone through anything like this? And to me, they were part of that dominant group that symbolized the status quo and oppression. Oppression might seem like a strong word, but I just mean part of the larger group of society that wasn't like me.

Because my family was my main support system, I also

103

was afraid that if I told them about the way I was treated, perhaps they would blame themselves in some way. We never discussed anything about being adopted, and I never raised any questions because I didn't want to hurt my mom's feelings. I knew she loved us, and I didn't want her to think she wasn't a good-enough mother or that I was trying to find out who my biological mother was. I didn't want her to feel threatened.

I didn't have any close friends who were Korean, and it wasn't until graduate school that I met other Asians. I had close girlfriends, but I felt like I couldn't talk with them about being adopted or anything like that. These feelings of being so isolated became quite a central part of who I am. Looking back, I don't think I really comprehended how much I didn't fit in. Even if I had, I know now that I never would have been able to articulate my feelings.

The majority of my high school friends were the kids others considered "weird and uncool" -- the ones dressed in plaid, wearing black nail polish, skateboarding after school and donning punk hairstyles. Their main interest was having fun and getting high on drugs and alcohol. I was looking for a sense of belonging. My being Korean or adopted wasn't an issue for them. They didn't really care, for the most part, because what we had in common was getting high which created a sense of community. I experimented with drugs, but because I was able to keep my grades up and continue with my extracurricular activities, my drug use went undetected. I can't believe I'm saying this, but I remember I took my ACT test while I was somewhat intoxicated from partying the night before. Because I did really well on the test, I figured, hell, I can do all these things, and I can still come out better than most kids who are at home doing their homework all the time.

So I continued doing that for the first year and a half of college. Then I stopped. A couple of friends of mine became addicts and one died. As I heard about acquaintances being incarcerated for possession of drugs or dealing drugs, I thought, I don't want to end up like that. I'm in college now, and these people that I hung out with are still bagging at the local grocery store. That seemed, well, fine for high school, but I was getting older, and started thinking, do I want to do this and work at the mall for the rest of my life? I realized it was time for me to grow up and to focus on my studies. I'm just very fortunate and very thankful that I grew out of that phase of my life.

My phone was by no means ringing off the hook from the boys calling during high school. Where I lived, interracial dating was not looked upon kindly. For example, a girl at my school dated an African-American boy and soon found her locker torn apart, with the words "nigger lover" written all over it. She was told that if she continued to see him, she would get beaten up. During my junior and senior years, I did date one classmate, a laid-back, not-popular, somewhat "out-there" guy with a good sense of humor -- the class clown. He never made comments about my being adopted or looking different from my adopted family. He seemed to accept me for me and didn't seem to care what others thought of him. He saw positive qualities in me that others overlooked because they didn't take the time to get to know me.

However, I felt that his mother did not accept me because I was not Caucasian. As our relationship became more serious, I wasn't allowed to come into their house. Every time I went there I wanted to scream out in anger when I was asked to sit in the car and wait for him. I never talked to him about his mother's attitude. I wasn't angry with him -- just embarrassed. I think I was embarrassed at being Korean because being different was not cool, especially to a teenager. I didn't want to draw any more attention to myself, and I think I was in denial about my identity and my background, so I tried to hide it or not talk about it. Then, at the beginning of our freshman year in college, we broke up. Besides the problem with his mother, we began to have our differences on life goals, politics, education and all sorts of things. His behavior began to change, becoming more power-oriented and verbally and physically aggressive toward me.

As I moved on in search of the right guy, I found out that there are men out there who have an Asian fetish. In slang terminology, these men are also known as "rice kings or queens," depending on one's sexual orientation. I find this type of fetish annoying and offensive. In my opinion these men are attracted to a stereotypical image of a partner who is submissive and exotic. I actually had a stranger come up to me and say, "I would love to have a girlfriend like you. My friend only dates 'Orientals' because they cook, clean, are good at sex and will draw a hot bath for their man."

My first instinct was to choke this man and watch him suffer, gasping for his last breath of air. Instead of drawing him a bath, I felt like drawing a noose around his neck. However, I refrained from doing so and instead, politely explained how that statement made me feel and why I was very offended. He gave me a blank stare and walked away. I have had several similar experiences on first dates, which, not surprisingly, doubled as the last.

College gave me my first taste of education outside parochial school. My classes in sociology, psychology and social work awakened me to the fact that I wasn't crazy or

106

alone in all my feelings of self-hatred and not belonging. I learned that those were common responses to racism, prejudice and discrimination.

During college, I made a few friends, people to eat lunch or have coffee with, and occasionally go out with to listen to local bands. Although there are a couple of people I continue to e-mail from time to time, my last years in undergraduate school were pretty lonely. My peers reflected the conservatism of the community, not questioning authority or thinking critically. I found most of them boring so I decided to immerse myself in my studies to prepare for graduate school.

During my graduate studies in social work I finally began to make sense of my Korean identity. Also, the university that I attended actively recruited international students, so I had an opportunity to meet people from different countries.

During my first semester, I became friendly with a colleague named Mark, who grew up in Seoul, but had previously studied English in the U.S. The Korean international students were envious of him because he was seen as more assimilated to American culture than they were, and therefore, more acceptable to Caucasians. Like me, Mark sometimes felt caught in the middle, or "marginal" as he would say -- not fully accepted by Koreans or by Americans. We had long discussions regarding our experiences with racism and discrimination, and what it was like to be "invisible." For instance, we had both stood in lines at stores, restaurants, bars and concerts only to be waited on last. Mark spoke to me about Korea and its people, culture and food. I was intrigued and excited, because I finally had met a Korean who accepted me and gave me information about my birth country.

For the first time, I felt I was in a culturally safe environment. There were many student groups within my program, but none for Asians. I wanted to do something about this, so my friend and I founded the Asian Pacific Islander Issues Association (APIA).

We planned activities dispelling the myths and stereotypes of Asian Americans and educating others on social work issues affecting the Asian population. We gained the respect of both our colleagues and faculty. By participating in this group, I was able to speak up in ways that I couldn't while growing up. I had the power to show others that we're not invisible. I was no longer the girl who knew something was different about her, but couldn't articulate it. I now could voice my views about how racism, politics and socialization affect the image and treatment of Asians in the United States. For the first time I was proud to identify myself as a Korean American. In fact, I feel privileged to have a multi-ethnic background.

As I moved into my 20s, the guys I dated all shared one thing in common: they never made stereotypical comments about my being Korean, nor did they ask personal questions about my cultural background. This was very important to me, as I wanted to be seen as a human being first. I ended up dating one person for nine years -- someone I met in college. Being Caucasian, he never knew, even though he tried, what it was like to experience the things that I did. Because we dated for so long and he saw the way I was treated, especially as part of a biracial couple, he thought he knew it all when it came to diversity. This attitude was irritating and frustrating which further compounded my feeling that no one understands me. Even though we were best friends, I evaded serious talks like this because I was afraid to expose deepest feelings of aloneness.

There was one time when we did have a discussion. He used to work in construction for his father in a small, conservative city, and one time he and his coworkers went to this little restaurant for lunch, still filthy and smelly from working outside. He remembered that people had given them dirty looks because they were so grubby. He said, "Oh, I know what it's like for people to stare, or for people to not want to sit by me." And I said, "You know, I'm glad that you see that, but you're fortunate that you can go home, take a shower and that dirt comes off, and you go on with your life. That's not the case for me or other people of color who don't have the automatic privileges that come with being a white male."

I think then, at some level, he understood me more than the average person. Yet he'd never been refused service in restaurants and stores or physically threatened and harassed because of the color of his skin or the shape of his eyes. I'm sure he couldn't imagine what it was like to be asked, "Do you eat cats and dogs because those are what 'your kind of people' like to eat, right?" These words came from people who were unrefined, uneducated, tobacco-chewing rednecks. Over and over again, I have had to say to others, "No, I do not know martial arts, karate, am not a tailor, mathematical genius or professional ice skater, nor do I own or work in a nail salon." At first, this type of oppression, ignorance and lack of respect was hurtful, but later, my hurt evolved into anger and cynicism.

Once when my boyfriend and I were vacationing in Florida, four men older than my parents surrounded me and made jokes about Japanese foreign cars being horrible products. These men were friends of my boyfriend's sisters

109

who were also with us. They said I was like a Japanese car in the U.S. -- worthless junk that should be sent back to the country I came from. The men proceeded to physically push me around and laugh. I told them I was not amused by their ignorance and walked away. My boyfriend's father overheard what was going on and told his son who replied, "She can handle herself." He was correct; however, I would not have minded if he had intervened. In situations such as this I have always been left to either defend myself or ignore the harassment.

Another incident happened a few years ago when I was at a convenience store purchasing a beverage in a small town in northern Michigan. The man working the cash register was very rude to me. Instead of handing me the change, he threw the coins at me, the metal disks bouncing off my body, scattering onto the floor. I turned around and walked out, refusing to bend down to pick up 37 cents in pennies and nickels.

I have remained silent so many times when faced with stereotyping, name-calling and discrimination. I used to be afraid to speak out or up for myself -- afraid of what might happen or what others might think. As I have grown older, I've learned that I have choices other than to stay quiet. By challenging myself to speak up, I challenge the belief systems of those around me. What others may perceive as aggression I see as freedom and assertiveness. I finally feel I am entitled to my feelings, without having to apologize. It's my way of saying I have been knocked down many times, but my injuries have made me stronger, and I refuse to perpetuate the Asian female stereotype.

In 1999, a month after I received my master's degree in social work, I visited Korea for the first time with a group of other Korean adoptees on a trip called "Journey," sponsored by the Korea Society. It was amazing to meet up with these individuals who grew up similar to the way I did. I thought this is going to be so cool. I'm going to Korea, and for the first time I'm not going to stick out because of my appearance. But when I got there, even though I was not physically salient, I felt like I am so American that it's not even funny. I could not believe how I still felt so different.

All of us felt that way because none of us could speak Korean. When we were walking around and Korean people spoke to us, I felt embarrassed because I didn't know the language. Communication with my host family was difficult because their English was very limited and I wanted to express to them how thankful I was for their hospitality. I wanted to tell them about my day, how exciting it was, and to ask them all the things I didn't understand, but I really couldn't do that. It was very frustrating, so we did a lot of charades, which took a lot of time. It was painstaking to use my elementary-level Korean vocabulary to describe all the awesome things I wanted to talk about. In fact, it was quite impossible.

Despite the difficulties, I wanted to just soak up as much as I could while I was there, to learn things I had never learned as a kid ... about life in everyday Korea. I learned how to eat with chopsticks, which is something I didn't do well before. The different smells and the food were very new, the heat and humidity were horrible, the bus rides were wild and erratic, but everything was just fascinating. My trip to Korea made me feel much more comfortable with being Korean American. This glimpse into my culture of origin validated my sense of self by filling in the blanks of what it meant to be Korean.

111

I came away with a feeling of relaxation and of contentment. Although I have a lot to learn about myself, the picture was becoming clearer and I was getting closer to coming around full circle. To me, Korea had become a real place with distinct meaning, versus the name of an unfamiliar country where I was born. (You don't come from an airplane!) I saw the people, ate the food, walked the streets, climbed mountains, and rode the buses and subway. I was excited to tell my family and friends about my new experiences. I spoke so much about it, that I thought, God, people are going to be so sick of hearing me say Korea this, Korea that. When I shared my experiences and pictures with my mother, she was totally into it. My home-stay mother surprised me by sending a hanbok, which I wanted but couldn't get while in Korea. I put it on and it fit perfectly and my mom was thrilled to see me in a traditional Korean dress.

We were too busy on the trip for anyone to do any kind of searching for birthparents. However, the tour guide introduced us to some people who wrote down our Korean names and birth dates, but it wasn't much to go on and it didn't appear to be a serious search. Interestingly enough, when I talked to other adoptees on the trip, they were all told the same story about being left on the steps of an orphanage -- or a police station. It seems unlikely that we were all abandoned in the same manner. I then wondered if our adoption agencies told all our parents a generic, scripted story.

A few years ago I asked my mom how she would feel about my starting a search and she said she would support me. I realized she was secure enough in our relationship not to feel threatened. I had been afraid that she would question my desire to search. I know I can go ahead and start the search but fear is holding me back. I am terrified to get the

112

ball rolling because not having any facts about my adoption protects me from anything negative or possibly disturbing about my birth family. Ignorance is bliss, but, at the same time, I know I will search. It is just a matter of being emotionally and psychologically ready to handle the good, the bad, or the disappointment of never finding them.

I've looked on the Internet at other people's search stories and there are positive -- and not so positive -- results. Some people have been searching for several years and come up with nothing. I would be really disappointed if that happened to me. I would also find it difficult to process negative or traumatic events. I have also thought, what if I'd found members of my biological family and they treated me poorly? For instance, I read stories of a few adoptees whose birth families wanted to come to the States or wanted money. If the adoptees couldn't or wouldn't agree to meet these expectations and do all that, the families made them feel guilty. Thinking about all of this makes me feel overwhelmed and question whether or not I want to begin a search.

Although I don't know anything about my biological mother, I have a lot of respect for her. I don't know what it's like to be pregnant, but I imagine it must be very difficult to make the decision to give a child up for adoption. I think her decision took a tremendous amount of bravery.

My biological mother has always been a positive thought in my mind. I think if she's alive, how difficult it must be for her to imagine how my life has been. I wonder if she keeps track of my age, wishes that I am safe, and hopes that I am happy. On my trip, every time I saw a Korean woman within her age range, someone who looked somewhat like me, I thought: What if she was my mom, and I would never know it?

Although I have become more secure in my identity,

113

it still can be a balancing act. For instance, when I look for a job and I put down I was born in Korea, people ask if I'm a citizen. Other times when people see or hear my last name, they're like, "How'd you get that name?" Sometimes I feel as though I have each foot in a different world -- one American, another Korean. Over the years I've learned that many people think the words "Caucasian" and "American" are synonymous. Therefore the most difficult part of being a Korean-American adoptee has been dealing with the perception among Caucasians that I'm a "foreigner" with little in common with other Americans. Ironically, my upbringing is a reflection of average America.

As I grow older, I realize more and more that struggling with issues of identity and self-acceptance has made me stronger and wiser. Gone is the time when I wished for blond hair and blue eyes. I am now able to accept those things about me that cannot be changed. Also, gone is my intense, endless effort to be completely understood by others, which I now see is an absurd expectation.

Now, I am grateful just to be me.

A.J. (Amy Jo) Thomassen, 34
Social Worker
St. Louis, Missouri

114

Jesse

For most of my life, I have never really considered myself Korean, or even Korean American. Searching for an identity has played a profound role in the development of who I am today. We all question who we are, where we fit in, and I am certainly no different.

I was born on March 1, 1970 in Chicago. According to my father, my birthparents were Korean students living in the United States. That's all I know about them. My mother and father, Susan and Dan Nickelson, adopted me at birth. There really hasn't been much of a discussion about their reasons why. I don't think a whole lot of thought was given to whether I was a Korean baby, a black baby or so forth. I just don't think that my parents thought about it at all, in terms of race . . . they just wanted a child, and they weren't really concerned much about physical differences, I suppose.

Both my parents are from the Midwest, from rural Middle America. My father grew up on a farm in Colorado, and was the youngest of six children. After completing a B.A. at the University of Colorado, he left for Ethiopia as a volunteer in the Peace Corps. Like my father, my mother grew up on a farm, but in Iowa. After matriculating from Macalester, and obtaining a master's degree from Michigan State, my mother ended up in North Carolina where she met my father, who was working on a Ph.D. in political science at the University of North Carolina, Chapel Hill, and volunteering in the civil rights movement. Eventually my parents moved to Chicago, where I was adopted. After living there for a year, we moved to Washington, D.C. where I grew up.

My parents have instilled a strong sense of fairness and courtesy in me, and I believe this stems from their Midwestern upbringing and their involvement in anti-poverty programs. Their experiences gave them enough courage to take on the challenges of raising a child in a society just beginning to embrace diversity

I first noticed the physical differences between my parents and me at a fairly young age. I used to stand on the edge of the bathtub when my father would shave at the sink, and I would kind of peer around the mirror and watch. I remember noticing that my eyes and his eyes looked very different. His hair was brown and thick and curly, while mine was jet black and straight. I asked him why we looked so different. He explained that I was adopted and I asked what that meant, and I don't remember his exact words, but he explained that my birthparents were Korean and that he and my mother had made me their son. I really honestly think I was 3 or 4 or

116

maybe 5, so it was one of those moments where the idea was kind of there for a minute and then I just got distracted by something else. I remember hearing the word "adoption" and I just kind of remember going, "Oh," in my head and that was about it. I have no memory of anything else, so I guess I didn't obsess about being adopted. These were my parents and this was my family, and to me, at least as a child, it seemed I was like anybody else with their family. It never really was something I thought twice about.

When I was 3, my younger brother, Joel, was born, my parent's biological son. Right before he was born I got a dog. Later, I believed that the idea was to distract me, but the latest info has it that my father really wanted a dog, and this was a great way to get one! Oddly enough, I also remember -- this is kind of funny, I think -- getting a kid's book on how babies are made. It became one of my more favorite books, which I think horrified my mom a little bit. I used to carry it around everywhere. I kind of enjoyed getting a brother, and we had a very good time as little kids.

I remember people always commenting on how much Joel looked like my parents. I didn't really see the similarity, mostly because he had these very deep blue eyes and this blond curly hair. Neither one of my parents has blond hair, but I guess my dad used to as a kid, and everybody, you know, really loved curly hair. One of my dad's favorite stories -- one he tells my wife all the time -- is that when my baby brother and I would take baths together, I would pour water over his head to make the curls go away so his hair would be just like mine. That's not just a story. I actually remember doing it.

My father distinctly remembers asking me, when I was about 5 years old, if I wanted to visit my ancestors in Korea.

117

Being a child, my response was, "Well, what about my brothers?" I guess I thought he was saying "and sisters," not "ancestors." I have a vague recollection of that, but for him it's a funny story that's as clear as day because, I suppose, it was one of those difficult questions to ask. And, he got an answer he was not prepared for. I don't think they did much of anything at that point, but sometime later I remember my mother asking me if I wanted to go visit Korea. This was another funny one . . . apparently my response was no, but I wanted to go visit the Caribbean.

As a young child I remember going with my mother to the Museum of Natural History and seeing an animation about a Korean prince. I can remember it clear as day being taken to see this movie, and having my mom kind of explain Korea. There was this evil god, it was a spider, and I can kind of still see it in my head. It was like a big deal when I was little, but then when it came down to, "Do you want to learn more?" it was kind of, "I don't know, whatever."

At the corner store near my elementary school was a market and the owners were Korean. They figured out I was Korean, and so one day they said some things to me in Korean. They were very nice about it, and I went home and apparently made some sort of statement about how I was glad I didn't live in Korea because I could never learn to speak the language! I was 7 or 8 and I actually remember being fairly resistant to anything Korean at that age. I kind of didn't want a whole lot to do with it because I wanted to be like everybody else.

Throughout my childhood and teenage years, I never changed my mind about going to Korea. It seemed that just looking Asian was causing problems for me in terms of "fitting in." Even though I had no understanding of Korean cul-

118

ture, I was seen as the perpetual foreigner. I think this led to a lot of missteps in school, beginning in the first grade when a Korean girl, who didn't speak English very well, entered my class. All of a sudden the teacher made me the girl's "buddy" and I didn't understand why. Now I can only assume that the teacher thought we would be comfortable together since we looked alike. I was told to help her out. While we were playing with clay, I was shocked as I watched her eat it! I tried to make her stop, but I could not communicate with her. I yelled out to the teacher, and then was scolded for letting it happen. I think my mom straightened it all out with a phone call to the principal, but from then on, I struggled to be as American as I could be. Being Korean seemed too difficult to "become" and in my mind, it was something that I was not.

Yet, when my friends and I played war games, I was always the bad guy -- the "Jap," the "gook," the "chink" or any other slur most people would dare not use today. At such a young age I had no context for those words. I just wanted to be GI Joe . . . to be what everybody else wanted to be. What bothered me was that I was always the enemy. Why? Because I looked the part. I have World War II, the Korean War, and the Vietnam War to thank for that. These kinds of interactions made me just not really want to deal with being Korean . . . part of it also was that it was just so foreign. I'd grown up here, and even by the time I was 5, 6 or 7, Korea was kind of scary to me . . . it was so different. I think part of it was a feeling like, what if Korean people decide they want to take me away from my parents?

My parents and I have a very close relationship now, but that wasn't always the case. I didn't want to be different from my parents or my friends. I mean I always got the sense, and I still have that sense, that both my parents, and particularly

119

my mother, have dealt with the differences between us by just never choosing to look at it that way. And, I think when I had some issues, particularly things that she didn't have experience with, I think it caused her a lot of stress. As an adolescent I made a point about our differences all of the time. Of course this is what most adolescents do anyway (speaking from a high school teacher's standpoint). There was one particular argument we got into a few years ago that really highlighted that problem in our relationship. There was a story about charter schools and I had a reaction to it, and she had a reaction to it, and they were kind of polar opposites . . . I kind of took a minority stance and she took a more pragmatic view . . . and in the end, I don't think either of us were wrong, but just looking at different parts of the problem. The reality of the situation was that I was upset that my point of view was not the first thing that popped into her head, and I resented that.

My mother explained to me that it was not fair to expect her to automatically see all my perceptions when she herself had never had the same experiences. It was the first time she basically let it be known that there are some things she doesn't have experience with in regards to race, and so for me to always expect certain responses wasn't always fair. As I look back over my life I realize that she has never had those kinds of expectations for me. I also know that my emotions sometimes have gotten the better of me. When I accuse people of being one sided in their views, I usually am doing the same from the other side. I also realize that all successful relationships require trust and understanding. Her big joke with me is that I am "intolerant of intolerance" . . . I need to be careful not to become that which I fear the most. Because of that argument I realize that my mother does see the differences between us, but she doesn't want them to come between us. I am her son. After that argument, things really changed for the better in terms of our ability to talk with one another.

There were times when being Korean got me into physical as well as verbal altercations. One day as a friend and I walked home from elementary school on a wintry afternoon, we were accosted by a group of high school boys. The snow had begun to fall before school let out, and it had piled up a couple of inches. About two blocks from home in what was then a quiet, almost-suburb of D.C., a car full of teenagers pulled up on the wrong side of the street. They all piled out of the car yelling. One of the boys screamed, "Kill the gook," and I remember thinking, "Oh my God, he's talking about me."

In an instant they threw us to the ground, stuffed snow in our faces, punched us in the stomach, and kicked us. I fought back, got violent and began screaming and crying. My friend Scott simply knelt in the snow and laughed hysterically, probably as a defense mechanism. One of the teenagers, who lived in my neighborhood, must have realized things were going very wrong so he called off the others and they got back in the car and left. Barely able to breathe, probably from laughing so hard, Scott asked why they did that to us. I told him I was not sure, but I felt it happened because I looked the way I did, and they did not like people who looked like me. In hindsight, it would be easy to say that it was boys being boys, and the racial component was secondary. And, although I would probably agree with this, I find the behavior repugnant.

My elementary school was predominately white, with a few African-American kids, but more African Americans

121

than Asians. Elementary school was not easy for me . . . it's funny, I went through this stage where I didn't want to go to school and it had to do with friends, not having enough, not being popular. Oddly enough my brother went through the same thing at the same age, so I don't know if that was learned, or if he just watched me do it, or if that's just something that happens at that age. Kids would make fun of me every now and then . . . I remember them making fun of things like my face, my eyes and the shape of my head.

I don't remember telling my parents but I do remember being asked if I had a problem . . . because I faked being sick for three days. I was upset, didn't like school, didn't have a lot of friends, and I never got the sense any of my teachers really liked me. I was never in the advanced reading or math groups in elementary school. I question that fact now because I have the standardized test scores from elementary school, and I was consistently in the 90th percentile in reading. Yet, I was never in the advanced reading groups. And then in the fifth grade my teacher yelled at me and made me cry in front of everybody. Not that it was a racial issue, but I just never felt I got the same attention as others, or got the same kind of support.

In junior high school I made a very big effort to be more accepted. I became very, very social. Oddly enough, all of a sudden one of the girls in my class thought I was cute. That had not happened in elementary school. Things snowballed from there . . . I was always on the phone -- to the point where my parents put a phone in my room. Then, in high school my parents even got me my own private line. (Big mistake!) I also had something else going for me -- tennis. I began taking lessons at age 10, and was competing within two years. In eighth and ninth grades I was a ranked tennis player in the

122

city and that absolutely increased my popularity, especially with the girls. Tennis gave me an identity. Playing sports was something positive that I could see definitive growth in.

It was also in junior high that I really began to learn about discrimination, and I began to have more in common with my black classmates than my white classmates. Although my school was located in the affluent, white quadrant of D.C., it drew a predominately black population from all over the city. My biggest problems stemmed from the "model minority" stereotype, something I learned all about in eighth grade.

Even back then, in the early '80s, I was aware of the stereotype that Asian kids were expected to know math and science . . . it was all over the news and I remember seeing a story about it in *Time* magazine -- how Asians were taking over the Ivy-League schools. I just didn't think anyone would apply the stereotype to me. I had never done well in math so, needless to say, I was not a stereotypical Asian kid. I was, in fact, a very stereotypical American.

One day in the eighth grade, there was an incident that pushed me over the edge. It was this incident that made me cynical and led me to believe that society would never give me a chance to succeed. I raised my hand to ask a question about the math problem on the board. The teacher became very angry, grabbed my desk with both hands, and yelled, "Do not ask any more questions!" Since she had never yelled at anyone before, I was shocked.

"You of all people should be able to do this!" she continued, then turned around and went back to the board. Well, her statement made no sense to me, so I just looked at her and said, "Why?" Of course she took that as a flippant comment, but then I started asking people around me, "Why should I know how to do this?"

No one would make eye contact with me. I became angry. "What did I do?" I asked the girl next to me. "Shut up. You're going to get me in trouble," she said. I was upset. "Why am I supposed to know how to do algebra?" I asked loudly to no one in particular. No one responded.

As the year wore on, I fell further and further behind. Eventually it was futile, and I began to fail. I spent most of the year sleeping in class, mostly to avoid feeling bad about myself. At parent conferences, the teacher would say that I would not show up for tutoring after school, but I'd never been offered it. I ended up taking algebra in summer school, passing with an A-.

For me, what solidified the whole episode as racially motivated was what happened the following fall when I enrolled in geometry for ninth grade. Unfortunately, I had the same math teacher who walked in, said "Good morning," saw me, and immediately her entire demeanor changed. She kind of sighed, slumped her shoulders, and said, "I'm sorry, there must be a mistake, you don't belong here." Those are the words I will never forget.

After opening a note from my counselor saying I could take the class, she gave me a dirty look and said, "Fine, but don't expect any help from me." I was crushed. I couldn't believe that was acceptable behavior for a teacher. I couldn't figure out what I had done to deserve this kind of treatment because I had done what everyone had asked. I had passed the class in summer school just to meet the prerequisite for geometry, yet this was the best I could get from a teacher. I passed geometry with a D-. How I did that I will never know. I always felt that she passed me so there was no danger in seeing me again the following year.

About four years later I felt vindicated when I heard she got fired for making another comment that was a little on the racist side. By then it was the late '80s and with political correctness coming about, you couldn't get away with saying stuff like that anymore

As I entered Wilson High School in the 10th grade, I had become a very angry young man. That anger would fester over the next three years. Many of my childhood friends who were white continued on in the upper track of the curriculum. One of my best friends since early childhood, who was my best man at my wedding, never had one class with me in high school. I began to feel cheated and discriminated against . . . I pushed away my parents, teachers and friends . . . I was on my own. There were a lot of problems with my friends from junior high school because increasingly, my classmates and my friends became predominately black.

I remember coming home one night after a party, and there were messages on my answering machine asking me why I thought I was black, and why do you act like a "nigger." Even a former girlfriend, who was white, showed me the ugly side of bigotry, linking my clothes and demeanor to black people. This incensed me even more.

I felt that certain doors were closed, and that no matter how badly I wanted them to open, it would never come to be. Sports became my release, my only hope . . . particularly tennis. It was the only thing I seemed to have control over and that sense of control was so strong that I often argued with the adults who tried to coach me. I became so disgusted with my high school coach that I did not play my senior year and turned to basketball. I did not realize it at the time, but I was setting myself up for failure.

I learned a great many things from my new friends in

125

high school. Some of those friends convinced me to join the Police Boys' Club basketball team, even though I had never played organized basketball. On the positive side, I became tougher. I traveled to parts of the city I never even knew existed. One of my best friends from junior high had convinced me to play on the team. That year he and I were two of only three non-black players in the league. We often drew a crowd when we played at other Boys' Clubs. People from that neighborhood would see us walking into the gym, and by halftime there would be a pretty good-sized crowd to see us play. While I had a couple of shining moments throughout the season, my friend had excelled into quite a basketball player. Later, as we continued to play on D.C.'s playgrounds, people would recognize us from that year in the league. That continued on into our college years. It wouldn't be a surprise to be walking through Georgetown and someone would say, "Hey, you guys used to play for No. 8 (Boys' Club)." While I was never a great basketball player, I learned to respect the game. It didn't really matter who you were, but if you could play and earn the right to be on the court, people would give you a certain amount of respect. And I relished the challenge of earning that respect.

The downside of my learning in high school was the anger and violence that I learned to use as a defense mechanism. I learned that fear was at the heart of discrimination, so I learned to show people why they should be afraid. Two wrongs may not make a right, but you sure as hell will feel better about yourself. I learned how to get by, not how to live. There was never a tomorrow. That meant I never had to plan, never had to be organized. I had a very narrow perspective about everything in life, but all of that would soon change.

126

I attended Rollins College, a tennis powerhouse in Florida, not for an education but to prepare to become a professional tennis player. Even though I did not play my senior year in high school, others convinced me that I had too much talent not to try out for the team. Rollins' program had seen a small number of players turn pro so it seemed like a perfect fit. I quickly realized that my training in tennis was lacking. Even though my college coach was impressed with my talent, he was baffled at my lack of thinking on the court. The dream of becoming a professional tennis player came undone at the beginning of my sophomore year. I was playing against a freshman for the last spot on the team. As the first set came to a close, I broke three strings on three different racquets. I panicked! Someone lent me a racquet, but I promptly lost the first set, and then the second. I was in a state of disbelief . . . and off the team. My entire reason for being in college was gone. After my meltdown, I was in counseling down in Florida . . . I was drinking an awful lot and ended up failing two classes and getting a D in a third.

I moved home, and took off the next semester. One of the best things that I did was to actually discuss with a counselor why I was the way I was and what that meant for my future. When the possibility of a professional tennis career fell apart, I was left with this kind of empty void of years of devotion to the sport and all the time spent . . . what did this mean for me now? It fit the pattern of all those superstars, not that I was much of a superstar, but all those athletes that never made it once they left high school.

During this time I was fortunate enough to work for Dr. Karen Rosenbaum, who owns and runs her own camp, TIC. The camp is a computer/athletic camp where children 7-16 years of age spend half the day learning how to program, and

127

half the day playing sports. We worked on developing the whole child and it was there I realized that I had a gift when it came to working with children. This was the first serious job that I had where I felt like my boss was working with me in my best interest. She became an invaluable mentor to me, and still is today.

TIC also exposed me to different people of different ages. Dr. Rosenbaum had always maintained a diverse staff, not just in terms of race, but people from all kinds of religious, international, and socio-economic backgrounds. I met many wonderful people who were very strong athletically and academically, and I began to benefit from their experiences growing up and dealing with school. That first summer I made some wonderful friends who strongly supported my new goals and my new direction.

I returned to Rollins motivated to get an education. For the first time in my life, tennis would not dictate the classes I could or would not take. After looking in the course catalog, I enrolled in "The History of Imperial China," taught by Dr. Charles Edmondson. I know that China is not Korea, but it seemed like a good place to start. Maybe I would find a connection to my ancestry that I had somehow evaded throughout all of my 20 years. Instead, I got much more than I ever bargained for.

Dr. Edmondson was one of the most popular and most difficult professors on campus. He would show up to class without notes and simply talk for an hour and 15 minutes, making Imperial China come to life. Listening to him was almost as good as watching history play itself out on television! For the first time in my life I was interested in going to class . . . looking forward to what would come next. I craved knowing why people would do the things he said they would do. I decided that I wanted to major in history.

But, I began to doubt my ability to pull this decision off. I was a 20-year-old young man who had given up on school in the eighth grade. I was not prepared adequately to do well in college. Until this point I had taken only one history class in college because the amount of reading would have interfered with tennis. I never took notes in class because it seemed like there was too much to write down and I never knew what was important. I had no real study skills, and I totally lacked command of the written English language. So, it was with great trepidation that I asked Dr. Edmondson to be my faculty advisor. He was extremely pleased that I wanted to become a history major, but confused by my concerns.

I told him about growing up in D.C. and how difficult life can be if you do not fit the right mold. And for me, it seemed that there never really was one. I was standing between worlds -- white, black, Asian. If I did not learn how to really read, write, and think at a college level, what future would I really have? Dr. Edmondson was stunned. I obviously had decent grades in high school, or I would not have been admitted to Rollins. I explained that I did what was necessary to stay eligible for sports, and that included cheating.

"When your back is against the wall and there only seems to be one way out, you take it," I replied. Almost on the verge of tears I tried to defend myself, explaining that I had turned a corner, and whatever happened I had to graduate college with a real education. After a long pause, Dr. Edmondson said that he would have to think about what I had just said. In a few days the college gave me another chance, but made it clear that my academic dishonesty could have been grounds for immediate dismissal. And if I slipped just once, I was out. I was overjoyed, relieved, and excited

129

all at once! I was given another chance, and I knew how rare an occurrence this was.

My focus shifted from China to Africa my junior year. We had a visiting professor, Catherine Higgs, who was a Ph.D. candidate from Yale in South African history. Since I had taken all of the classes that focused on Asia (three at the time) I decided to learn more about Africa, the continent that had defined a major part of the culture that influenced me growing up in D.C. To do this, my professor helped me develop a proposal to travel to Africa for a month on an independent study -- something no one at Rollins had ever done before. It was in Africa that I really began to find and define myself.

I traveled through Morocco and Ghana for a month. I do not know what I thought I was going to see or experience, but it was unlike anything I could have imagined. Oddly enough, my ethnic identity became one of the bigger issues in my research. People who were friendly (and some who were not) always tried to guess where I was from and then say something nice in that language. Most people in Morocco thought I was Japanese. I did notice that Sony, Hitachi, and several other Japanese companies had billboards everywhere in Casablanca. When I would reply in English, most people's eyes would get wide and they would say, "Oh, you are American."

After this happened a few times, I asked, "What makes you say that? Why American?" I received a variety of answers. "You just look American" . . . "You walk like an American, full of confidence" . . . "You speak like an American" . . . "You sound sure of yourself" . . . "You are always smiling like an American." These were responses that I got from Morocco to Ghana.

For the first time in my life I felt like an American. But, it's a feeling that I often did not get back home. For the Moroccan or Ghanaian I was an American because of who I was and how I acted, not based on any racial stereotype. Traveling abroad had given me a new direction in defining myself.

Upon returning to school, I continued to work hard in all my classes. Even though I had finally made the Dean's List, parts of my past refused to go away. One day while sitting in a friend's dorm room, a group of students came looking for me. They had a copy of my high school transcript, which I had apparently left in the library. I had asked for it to give myself a better perspective on how far I had come. The guys were upset because they had friends with better GPAs than I had in high school, who did not get into Rollins. They wanted to know how I got into the school.

Angry comments about affirmative action began to rain into the room. Admittedly, I felt a little guilty. I always presumed I was admitted because the tennis coach, who had three national championships, had really wanted me to play for the school. I also figured that being a minority did not hurt either. Before I could say anything, my friend told them to get out of his room. They wanted to know why he was upset, particularly since he did not really support affirmative action. He stated, rather loudly, that in principle he disagreed with affirmative action, but that if there was any case to be made for it, I was it, saying, "He has done more here with his education in one year than any of you have since you got here." My mouth dropped open. I didn't know what to say, except "thanks."

It was nice to know that someone else was paying attention to all my hard work. I earned a 3.3 GPA during

131

my last 36 credit hours. As I became a better student, I also became angry about the quality of my secondary education, and the low standards that had been set for me in school and on the tennis court. I decided that I wanted to return home and become a teacher so that I could really prepare students for success, rather than just stand around hoping that they would make it. To do this I had to go to graduate school at the George Washington University and get my master's in education and teaching certification.

While I thought being a minority in college was difficult, I was in for a shock in graduate school. I will never forget my first day. I put on a comfortable pair of jean shorts, a T-shirt, and a baseball hat (backwards, of course) and headed off to GW. I walked into the orientation and promptly turned around and walked out. Everyone in the room was dressed up! Some in coats and ties! I double-checked the room number and slowly walked back in, picked up my materials, and sat in the back, knowing that I was sticking out like a sore thumb. My clothes weren't the only problem. Out of 56 people in the room only three were minorities. So much for the "model minority" theory! Fortunately, I met Michael, an Irish Catholic from Syracuse, New York on the second day of class. He would keep me sane throughout my graduate school experience.

Very quickly I became frustrated . . . a couple of individuals were not only ignorant, but also racist, homophobic, misogynistic, and mean. Only Mike and I would openly challenge some of this thinking. Having personally experienced teachers not even trying to understand students, I grew more appalled as class went on. What upset me the most was the lack of intervention by the faculty toward racist comments by one student in particular. He was everything

132

that you would never want in a teacher. I met with the professor and went on a long diatribe attacking the student and the faculty's apathy. I told them it's painful for me to see that you're going to certify this guy to teach.

That's an area of concern, they said, but unfortunately it's about freedom of speech. After some reassurance that they'd take my observations seriously, Mike and I left. When we got to the elevator I commented that I'd gotten a little angry but overall the session went well. "Are you kidding?" Mike replied. "I've never seen anything like that. Do you realize every other word out of your mouth was a curse word?"

My mouth dropped open. I couldn't believe it and then, it hit me. Why didn't they say anything? Mike and I could only conclude that since no one else in the program had my background, I was simply allowed to express myself (in private, of course) in a way I was comfortable.

After getting my master's degree in 1995, I started teaching world history at the Benjamin Banneker Academic High School, a public high school in D.C. Banneker is a predominately black, college-prep program with students from all over the city. This assignment was not what I had been preparing myself for. I was looking to save lives in a war zone, convincing kids that they had more talent than they were being led to believe. Instead, I was confronted by students who were all highly intelligent and angry. During my first year I wondered if I would stay or move on to work in a school with larger problems. My TaeKwon-Do instructor helped me make the choice. "You may have been looking to save lives," he said, "but now you have the opportunity to mold leaders." That was enough to make me stay.

During my first year teaching, I rode my bike down to

133

Georgetown. I was on the sidewalk, and I came up behind this elderly couple. I was getting ready to warn them that I was passing on the left when all of a sudden the husband saw me. He moved toward me and pulled his wife with him. I stopped and said, "I'm sorry," and the lady turned around, hit me with her purse and cursed, "You Japanese people . . . you're always sneaking up on us Americans." Then she spit on me.

At that point, I just started yelling at her, and I could see the husband was beside himself like, oh my God how did this happen, and he's trying to pull her away, and I was extremely upset and again, nobody who saw it said a word to me or to her. I have the sense, at least, that if I see something that's really, really wrong, I'm going to show some support to the person who's being treated unjustly, maybe not intervene, but at least let them know they're not alone. It was one of those things where you just want to hit somebody, but then if I had hit somebody, I'd go to jail, and I'd be in trouble . . . I just was upset because I wanted to know what the penalty was for somebody who expresses themselves like that lady. I went to a friend's house and vented. He didn't have an answer but he was a good listener.

When I told my students the story, their eyes got all wide, perhaps because even though racism was a hot topic, they always said they'd never met a racist. "You weren't angry?" they asked, perhaps because I told them I didn't strike back.

"I was extremely angry and as a matter of fact, I'm still angry now, but there's a larger war to be won than just how I feel about this one lady," I told them.

I've thought a lot about this kind of situation . . . my reactions, my anger and how it all ties in with adoption. But, I can't find the tie. I just don't see it. I've just never been able to draw anything conclusive at all.

Teaching at Banneker has certainly taken my life in new directions. Not long after I started, one of my students, a Nigerian American, insisted I meet her sister, to the point of writing down her phone number and slamming it on my desk. Before this I had mostly dated white women . . . not really any Asians . . . it was just very comfortable . . . my parents were white and the neighborhood I grew up in was white and I'd been around white people for the majority of my life. By the time I got into college, that had changed a little bit because my peers in high school were primarily black. I began to think and feel that white women, although they face many similar issues, did not understand the stress and pressure of being a racial minority in this country. A lot of the women I dated, and I hate to use this stereotype, because not all white women would do this, but the ones I dated had a tendency to trivialize some of the things that I did not like about society. I tended to have a sense that there was just a lack of understanding for things that were difficult for me in terms of race. In many instances those girlfriends put pressure on me of a different sort. One even said that she didn't see me as Korean or Asian, but as someone who is white. I didn't like that either.

When I met my student's sister, there was a sense that she understood a lot of these issues. After dating for three years, we got married. We're an awful lot alike, which people don't always see. People look at us, and they're like, "Wow, that's just incredible," but when you really get to know the both of us, we understand certain things culturally, having grown up in the city, that bond us together pretty well. When we were dating, there were things about me that would just kind of throw her off, like the fact that I like chicken wings

135

and mambo sauce. That's because of Boys' Club basketball . . . you got a wing box with mambo sauce and you went and played basketball.

My wife and I had our first child, Laila, in May, 2003. At two weeks old, she looked just like me. However, both my wife and I are aware that she might go back and forth physically over the next several years. We are both excited about having a beautiful daughter. We decided to forego ancestral names because we are afraid of confusing her. After all, she is an American. I have spent a lot of time preparing for this moment, and I've made it a point to find people my age or in college who are biracial, and to try to get to know them very well. I've met some very impressive people and out of all the people I've spoken to, particularly the women, race, or their cultural identity, was not something that their parents allowed them to be ashamed of. One of these people is a former student of mine, Siu-Lin, whose father is African American and mother is Chinese American. I have had many wonderful conversations with her about finding her identity.

Another friend of mine who is a biracial woman told me that she had never met a racist. Actually, it wasn't that she hadn't experienced racism, but because of how she grew up, she just hadn't realized that she had. In many ways, I think it was to her benefit that she was unaware of people's ideas about her until she was old enough and mature enough to understand how she felt about it. It also gave her plenty of time to build an identity that was strong and secure, and that couldn't be eroded or inhibited by racist ideas.

I think there's a certain period in kids' lives, maybe between 7 and 15 or 16, where they should be protected from racism so their confidence, their self-esteem, isn't worn away. The eternal question is always -- how do we protect kids

136

while still allowing them to grow, experience and overcome? Today, I think society is much more aware of these issues than when I was in school.

Until I started teaching, I had spent a good portion of my life detached from Korea, its culture, and its traditions. I never even really saw many Koreans until at one point in college a woman I was dating had a male friend who was Korean. We got to know each other, and there were times when people would confuse the two of us somehow, and I really didn't understand that, although in certain instances, when we were laughing, I think you could say we looked like brothers. As we got to know each other, he got all excited about taking me back to Philadelphia to meet all his friends and family. For me it was a little too much too fast. What made me uncomfortable was any sort of expectation Korean people had of me . . . I was very, very worried about disappointing people because I didn't even know how to say hello, much less anything else in Korean.

Then, in the middle of my first year at Banneker it all broke loose. My seniors were completely confused by me . . . they had no idea what was going on, why I was the way I was, why I talked the way I did, why I acted the way I did. A couple of kids came up and asked at lunchtime, "What is the deal with you, because people are saying that you're adopted." I said, "Well, they're right." But, it turned out the kids assumed I had been adopted by a black family.

So, I spent a whole day in my classes, just discussing it and a kid finally asked, "What about learning about Korea?"

"Well," I told them, "I just haven't really taken the time and I really never had the interest." This young lady who was sitting in front, who's extremely bright, made this sound, and

137

said, "Well, I don't agree with that."

Most of my kids were shocked. "You don't really have a place to be disagreeing with him at all, it's his life," was one retort. But the student replied, "No, I have an opinion, and my opinion is that even if he is adopted, he's got an obligation to understand where his ancestors come from."

After listening to all of this I said, "Well, I can understand that, but the honest truth is, I don't really have a feeling for that, but it's something I'll consider." That was enough to appease her at that point.

Two years later, three black students were planning to travel to Korea through Project Bridge, an intercultural outreach program of the Korea Society. After a training retreat, some of them came into my room speaking Korean. "Annyong-haseyo!" (hello) After I gave them a blank look, put up my hands and told them to stop, they told me I had no choice but to join the program. So, I became part of Project Bridge 1999.

That trip with my students was just enough to whet my appetite. Eventually I ended up getting the Intercultural Outreach Program Fellowship to go back to Korea for 10 weeks to study Korean language at Yonsei University in Seoul through the Korea Society.

My goal was to claim the heritage of my ancestors by starting to learn their language. That was easy to say, but I honestly did not know if claiming my heritage was even possible. I was worried that Korean people might see me as something different . . . that they might not accept me because I could not speak Korean and did not know their cultural values. Yonsei provided me with the best foundation for learning Korean that I could have ever wanted. After having class for four hours a day, speaking no English at all,

138

my brain actually started thinking in Korean! This is one of the most exciting things that has happened in my life.

At first Seoul seemed overwhelming because of the language difficulties. I was afraid to get on the subway for fear of getting lost and never finding my way home! But, after three weeks of training and practice with schoolmates, all of a sudden I could read all the signs and listen in on conversations! I could buy just about anything and even ask for directions. It was like a giant shroud had been lifted and I could see. As my ability to speak improved, I became much more adventurous, visiting different parts of Seoul and getting a taste of what the city had to offer. My visits also took me to many places outside of Seoul, the most beautiful being the island of Cheju with its wonderful weather, beautiful mountains and beaches, and fantastic waterfalls. It was there that I surprised my girlfriend by asking her to marry me -- in the Korean language -- in one of the most beautiful spots in my ancestral homeland! My hope is that my children and grandchildren will always feel compelled to visit this place where my wife and I chose to begin our lives together.

One of the biggest highlights of my stay in Korea focused on people. I made many friends from all over the world . . . most saw me as an American more than anything else. Out on the street, however, things were very different. This was important for me to discover because I felt like I was sticking out like a sore thumb, when in fact I was blending in very easily! Most Koreans seemed confused that I did not speak Korean very well, while some of my friends of Irish or Anglo descent were pretty fluent. When a friend asked for directions, a Korean gentleman was so overwhelmed to hear a white American speaking Korean that he jumped in the air, making a funny sound of surprise. Bewildered, the gentleman turned and began speaking Korean to me. When my friend explained that I did not speak Korean well, the man jumped again and began looking back and forth between us as if we were playing some sort of joke. Eventually he just began to laugh, gave us directions and was on his way. In most cases, people seemed surprised at my difficulties with the language and supportive of my attempt to learn. In some rare instances, people refused to carry on a conversation if I couldn't speak Korean, but most were simply curious. When I explained that my parents are Americans who don't speak Korean, the usual response was, "But, you look like a Korean person!"

Sometimes I do wonder about my looks -- whether I resemble my birthmother or father, but I don't think I want to search for them. I don't really know. I've thought about this extensively and I have an issue with it, because if I searched, all of a sudden my life would have to split in two. And, I'm very comfortable with my life as it is, and so it's kind of like opening Pandora's box -- you're not quite sure what's going to come out of there. But, I do kind of have an interest in my family health history. Were my parents prone to cancer, diabetes or this or that? I'm hoping in my lifetime that gene-mapping will become reliable so that you'll be able to just take DNA and figure out if you're predisposed to some of these things. But, other than that, I also think about the flip side of the coin -- the fact that finding my birthparents could cause a certain amount of upheaval in their lives as well. So I'm kind of very comfortable with doing things the way I have. To me, searching people out feels a little uncomfortable.

If I were to become very famous or something, there might be a whole bunch of people saying, "Hey, that's my son." But, I don't know. I think when I've talked to people in Korea about it, there was a question of well, you know, those that went looking at least wanted to let their biological mother know that they were okay. And, I could kind of understand that, but at the same time, I don't really know what that must feel like for a parent, to see your child leave, come back and leave again. I'm not so sure I would like that.

I now have a vivid picture of the people, the land, and the culture of my ancestors. I have a better understanding of Korean people and their culture. I have begun one of the first steps of claiming my heritage by learning how to read, write, and even speak in Korean. My perception of who I am and where I come from has grown exponentially, but the picture's still not clear, at least to me.

However, in Korea I did meet at least one person who doesn't share my confusion. During my last night in Seoul, I was invited to dinner at a friend's hasuk jip (boarding house). I had dinner and a wonderful conversation with my friend's Ah ju ma (auntie). Like most other Koreans, she was perplexed with my inability to speak very well, and that my American friend Ted spoke the language much better than I did. After we explained my adoption by American parents she told me to thank my parents for her, for having such big hearts and taking a little Korean boy into their family. After dinner and some pictures we said goodbye. She took my hand, gave me a hug and said, "No matter what anyone else says, always remember, you are a Korean."

A few years ago, during my last summer as a counselor at TIC, I met a Korean adoptee there. He was 14 and very active, much like I was at that age . . . always where he shouldn't be. I have a tendency to think there is a dynamic between adoptive parents and kids . . . one that's true for any race, where parents want to make sure the kid feels loved, so they don't want to come down too hard sometimes. That means that the kid thinks there are no boundaries . . . that he can do whatever he wants.

Anyway, I'd seen this particular kid before, but I never put his name together with his face. It's an American name, an Anglicized name. So one day, he was being picked up early, and we were in the gym, shooting baskets, waiting for his parents to get there, and I just said, "I gotta ask you about your name. It sounds like an American name, kind of like mine." I was like, "You're looking at me the same way I'm looking at you."

"Yeah," he said, "I'm adopted."

And I said, "Me, too."

Jesse Lucas Nickelson, 37
High school teacher
Wheaton, Maryland

팔 Kathleen

To the best of my knowledge, I was born in Seoul. I was in an orphanage since infancy so I'm a little unclear about the facts, but I believe that in the first couple months of my life, I was abandoned and found in the Dong-du-moon area of the city. I stayed in an orphanage until I was adopted when I was about 20 months old.

My birthday is April 27, 1961, but that date and also my name, Lim, Ja Sook, were given to me by the orphanage. I know that they're not correct because I came with no identifying information. The orphanage told my parents that the birth date was estimated through dental records, and because I was so young when they found me, I'm sure that's pretty accurate, pretty close.

At the time of my adoption, I

143

was considered a failure-to-thrive baby, not walking, not speaking, not eating solid food and all those things, so there were certainly some developmental delays. My parents had previously adopted my non-biological brother, Mark, from Korea and they also had two biological children, Bob and Kris. They were living in Hawaii at the time, receiving newsletters from Holt International, and they saw my picture with a group of children who really needed to be adopted and decided to go ahead. My sister had wanted a sister, and so that was part of the motivation as well. My father, a Lutheran minister, had a parish in Hawaii at the time, and my mother was a homemaker, so I grew up in a pretty traditional Caucasian family, at least from the outward description.

I think my parents' motivation to adopt was very different from that of people who adopt because they can't have biological children. After all, they already had two children when they adopted Mark, as an infant, about a year and a half before me. I think they really did it because they believed in human rights, certainly from a spiritual, religious standpoint, and believed in the need to practice what they preached as far as caring for people. They also wanted to add to their family and they didn't see any reason to have more biological children.

After I was adopted in Hawaii, my parents stayed there for another year or so, then went back to California for a short time, and then moved us to India for four and a half years where my father taught at a seminary. Living in India was an amazing experience for me because I was immersed in a situation where I was still a minority, but it wasn't a predominately white society. My siblings and I went to boarding school at a very young age, starting in first grade. The school was probably about a half-day's drive from where my parents lived. It was up in the mountains, an international boarding school with a lot of missionary children, but also children of business people who were in India for different reasons, and diplomats. It was very, very diverse. So I had friends who were Hindu and Buddhist, and friends actually from all over the world.

After India we came back to the States, to Minnesota, for about six months, and then went to England where we lived for another four and a half years. In England my father worked for World Missions, for the theological education fund. When I was in eighth grade we came back to the U.S., to Columbus, Ohio, where I completed high school.

I've always been aware that I'm adopted. Obviously when you're an interracial adoptee, you only have to look in the mirror and you realize that you are, but I don't think that I really understood, especially when I was living in India. I just came to a realization that everybody was different in different ways, and I had my own uniqueness around that, but it wasn't until we moved to England that I really had a sense that being different wasn't acceptable. Moving into a predominately Caucasian environment was kind of a shock for me. When we were in boarding school in India, I really don't recall being teased much for being Asian. But, when we were in the school system in England, I clearly remember my brother Mark and I both being teased. A lot of what would happen was basically my brother, in particular, getting teased and asked constantly if he knew karate or kung fu.

We were raised at a time where most people, most school children, certainly didn't know what Korea was or where it was. All they knew was China and Japan, so they would always ask my brother if he knew karate and, you know, get in front of him and try to pretend they were trying to do karate to him. He finally got to the point where they would ask him and he would say yes, and then they would leave him alone, so it was that sense of sort of being harassed about it. I got teased a lot, like people would pull their eyes and say "ching-chong" and that kind of stuff to me or make those kind of comments. That was pretty run of the mill. Usually it's the kids that you don't know well that do that, but I still think that even your close friends will make jokes. At one level it doesn't bother you as much because they're close friends and you have a relationship with them, but at another level it does, because they should know better. It kind of creates a sort of interesting conflict.

At that age, you just want to be like everybody else, so the teasing was upsetting. Luckily, my parents were very good at teaching us to accept the fact that when people say ignorant things, it's about them, not about us. It's about their lack of knowledge, not about something that's inherently wrong with us. Of course, as a young person, it's one thing to know . . . it's another thing to be able to really start integrating that in, and not feel bad. I definitely went through a stage where I wanted to be white.

My father is very much the traditional, and he's a scholar, not aloof, but very intellectual. My mom was really the nurturer in our family, so she was very good with all four of us kids about having a real sense of open communication and talking about adoption issues . . . it was never anything that had to be whispered about. We used that language since the day we could start speaking, really, and it was clearly acceptable to talk about differences and about being adopted, so I think that felt safe to me.

Because my brother and I are both Korean and only six months apart, we were pretty much raised as twins, even though we're very different in the way that we see things -- through high school he was certain that he wasn't Korean, and was very unwilling to talk about being different, so it's sort of interesting because we come from the same environment.

I really see my parents as being forward thinking for their generation. At the time that they were raising us, you know, it was in the '60s and the early '70s, and my parents were always very vocal and active supporters of the civil rights movement, and so they really truly socialized us to be aware of social justice issues and to talk about race and to talk about differences and to recognize the racism that does occur in our society. When it came down to our personal experiences, my mom would sort of just listen and ask, "What do you think you could do differently or how did you respond?" I don't think she did a lot of intervention and from my estimation, that's important because I think kids need to learn to develop their own coping skills and not have their parents rescue them from those kind of things.

My parents didn't do anything to immerse us in Korean culture, but I think that was more a function of not having the opportunity. When we lived in India, there wasn't a Korean community and when we lived in England, there wasn't either, or not that I was aware of, but my father had a colleague who was a Chinese woman, and she was very instrumental for me because she spent a lot of time with our family and when she would come over to the house, she would always make the time to sit and talk with me and Mark. She's the one who taught me how to use chopsticks, and she would take us to cultural things, if ever anything Korean came through London. I remember very clearly when she took me to go see the Little Angels, which was a traveling Korean

147

dance troupe of young people and that was the first time I'd ever seen traditional Korean dance. So, this woman was very significant by being a role model for me but she wasn't in my life that long. It was more of a transitory thing, but she definitely made an impact because she made me sort of able to experience myself as Asian American.

Back in the '70s when we moved to the States, Holt was having culture camps, and my parents did tell us about it, but I don't think Mark and I were interested. During the summer after my junior year of high school my parents also offered to send me to Korea for cultural immersion at one of the universities. I had expressed an excitement about doing it, but when the time got closer, I backed down.

I think my parents wanted to send me because it was very normal for me to have conversations about being Korean and experiencing being Korean, wondering out loud what it was like to be in Korea . . . certainly when we got back to the States, we went to Korean restaurants when we could. But, when I actually was given the opportunity to go to Korea, I didn't . . . I think it was more because I would have gone by myself. I think if my family had gone, I probably would have . . . I was thinking, oh, I'm going to be in a different country all by myself. It was just too scary for me. At that time, there were no group tours of adoptees going to Korea.

In high school and middle school it's natural to develop social cliques, an interest in dating and what not. The message that my brother and I both got from our peers, very clearly, was that it was okay for us to be friends with people, but dating was another situation. I was very aware of it and I'm sure my brother was, but we didn't talk about it. I was very aware that I could be friends with guys, and I could go out in groups, but when it came down to dating, it just wasn't going to happen.

When I did date, it was usually somebody who wasn't going to my school, someone a little bit older. I got the sense that somehow this was a huge leap for the person I dated, you know what I mean, like a huge concession. It wasn't articulated, I just got the sense that he was being defiant or whatever . . . there were conversations that went, "Well, I don't care what other people think . . ." There was definitely that sense that dating me was outside of the norm.

As far as my brother was concerned, he didn't date, but he did group things, like we both went to proms and stuff because we were in the same grade. When girls would talk about my brother, they would say, "Oh, he's so cute," but it was very patronizing, like he was a puppy. He was rather short by white American standards, only 5'6" or so, so that didn't help.

Having a brother who was also adopted from Korea helped me from the standpoint that when I entered new situations, I wasn't by myself. But, it was really more than just that. Because Mark was Korean as well, we almost single-handedly, you know, integrated our high school. That felt safer for that reason, but my brother didn't talk about being adopted or what it meant to be a Korean, and so we never had those conversations . . . there wasn't a lot of support or connecting. It was just his presence that made a difference to me.

I find it somewhat humorous that Mark couldn't talk about these things, but I also think that he was just dealing with his differences in the way that he knew how. He would say things like, "Well, I'm not any different than anybody else. I just look different, I'm just as white as everybody else." It cracked me up. I don't think his opinion is any less

149

valid than mine. I just think that he was a little naïve, that's all. I would get frustrated at him, not angry

He found acceptance by being involved with sports. For guys, sports just seem to be this sort of leveling thing, and he was very good, so that made a big difference. But, I think I've always felt like he was in denial on this and at some point, he was going to have to deal with those issues. Now in his 40s, he is . . . slowly.

It's interesting because he adopted both of his children from Korea. That has made such a difference in the way he sees the world . . . it's not just having children, but knowing that they have to navigate the experiences that he did, wanting to protect them from that, or equip them better for it somehow. So he's gotten involved in these culture camps, something he would never have gone to himself, but he's taking his kids to them and it's really, really interesting. He and his wife were unable to have biological children so I guess it was just like a natural inclination for them to adopt from Korea.

I was married when I was 20 and had completed two years of college. I had met my ex-husband when I was a senior in high school. Part of the reason I got married so young was because my father is a Ph.D. and very, very intelligent, and I think I felt a lot of pressure to be successful and had a fear of failure if I didn't do well. My parents did not articulate these expectations -- they were more self-imposed and I suppose it was easier for me to quit than fail.

My now ex-husband is a year older than I am and was in college when we met. I have always liked to help people, and I was sort of drawn to people who needed me. When you're 20 years old, that's kind of appealing, but when you're older, it's not. Anyway, we married. He was from a very small

150

town in Ohio, very insulated. His parents and grandparents struggled with issues of race and how to be comfortable with me as a daughter-in-law, but we married and then I had my twin boys in 1982, right before my 21st birthday. They were two months premature and so that kind of made a decision for me about whether I was going to be able to complete college right away. At the time, my ex-husband was in the Air Force, so we lived in Colorado when the kids were born, far from our families. You grow up really quickly when you're responsible for somebody else.

When the twins were 4 years old, I was pregnant with their brother, Alex. He was born full term and healthy in 1986, but he died of crib death a few months later. After Alex died, knowing that I wanted to adopt, I decided to go ahead and start the paperwork. My daughter, Brittany, came from Korea in 1988 when she was 3 years old.

When my children were growing up I worked pretty much all the time in administrative support jobs. I completed my undergraduate degree in '91 and my master's in social work in '94, the same year my husband and I divorced. It was my decision. I think there were certainly a lot of reasons, but one of the major contributing factors was the death of our son. That was a very life-changing moment as far as our relationship was concerned, the way we grieved differently, and the way we sort of moved forward differently. I never consciously found any fault in that my ex was home when my son died, but I think for me there was some anger around that, not that I blamed him, but just the way he dealt with it.

I always think it's interesting how when adoptees think about birth family, they always think about birthmothers, and they don't think about birthfathers. That would be an interesting research topic. I guess I didn't think of my

151

birthfather at all, but in a way I did. For me it's always been more of a physiological thing . . . you know, who do I look like? Your biological children talk about who do they look like and how they got this or that from somebody, even their temperaments. How much is hereditary and how much is environment? So, my curiosity was really about various tangible, physiological things. I never had these fantasies like some people I hear about who imagine that their mother was a princess or whatever.

There wasn't a particular moment when I sat down and asked my parents about my birth family, or when they sat down and told me. It was always just open information and what my parents told me was my story as they knew it, that I was abandoned and that there was no information about my birthparents. I don't have my birthmother's name. The only information I have is where I was found and the date.

When I was in Korea in the summer of 2003, I did go to Holt and actually, even before that, I did contact the agency to see if they had any information. They sent me what they had in their file, and it was very little, so when I went to their office in Korea I asked to see my file. While I knew that there wasn't going to be much, I was a little taken aback by my experience because the social worker was clearly uncomfortable. When she was talking to me, she said, "I don't know how to tell you this, but we've lost your file." And I said, "What do you mean you've lost my file?" Apparently because I was adopted so long ago, and with the movement of files from one place to another, they didn't have it. So what they gave me was sort of a recreated file.

With some adoptees I know that sometimes they've been told there's no information in their file, but eventually that turns out not to be true. So I always had that little piece

152

of hope, but of course, the information wasn't there, so that was very discouraging. And I have thought, although there's a lot of feelings of ambiguity around this, that I should do some sort of public search, you know, whether it's putting an advertisement in the paper or whatever. I know there are a lot of venues to do that in Korea, but I have mixed feelings. There's such a strong chance that it's going to net nothing. The amount of emotional and logistical energy, of getting somebody to translate, and figuring out how to contact a Korean newspaper . . . it's just going to require a lot of energy. And my fear is that it's going to come to naught, so do I really want to expend that energy? I think my greater fear is of not finding anything. I did actually talk to one of my colleagues at the university who's a Korean American and in communications. He offered to help me, but when he found out how little information I had, he really felt like I wasn't going to be able to find anything.

In the summer of 2000, I visited Korea as a social worker. I was traveling with a group that brings adoptees and their families on birth country tours. It was my first time in Korea since I was 5 years old when my family passed through Korea on our way to India. To be traveling as a professional was challenging because I was actually experiencing what the tour group was experiencing, yet I was supposed to be there as the emotional support for them.

When I first got there, it was this amazing thing. You have this awareness that you've been there before, you've done this before, but in the reverse direction. I really felt like I was coming home, I mean I really did. Walking off a plane and seeing people that looked like you was just a very amazing feeling . . . very powerful. Being in Korea, it's different, part energizing, part weird, feeling at home, feeling very congruent.

As much as adoptive parents try to discount it, I realized during the trip just how much race is a factor in adoption. One experience that emphasized this was when I was with the adoptive parents and their families on the beach. I don't remember where it was, but there was this woman who was trying to sell her wares, and she was being very insistent. I was sort of telling the kids to tell her no, and even though the parents knew I'm an adoptee and they knew I was raised in the States and they knew I don't speak Korean, they said, "Kathleen, can you tell her . . . " They wanted me to translate.

It was just so funny because as supposedly aware and sensitive of the position that their children are in as adoptees, the parents still, when they were uncomfortable, reverted to that sort of visceral response . . . any Korean face would do . . . just come here and translate for us. It was so interesting.

I think most adoptees -- at least I'll speak for myself -- come back with this sense that we need to learn Korean and the trip sort of renewed my energy about learning Korean. That's something I really struggled with because I really understand that culture is carried through language, and that the only way you can understand a culture is if you understand the language. But, when you get into your real life, then you realize that it's really hard to learn because the Korean language is not very accessible in a lot of the U.S.

When I adopted Brittany from Korea it felt like a full circle for me. I mean it was something I always knew I wanted to do, and it just felt right, natural and it was like something that was a very positive experience for me. I get this question a lot because maybe I'm raising my children differently than my parents did. I've tried to get Brittany

154

involved in doing Korean things. To me, and this reflects my writing a lot, it's not about doing things, it's about being. My daughter has the, I think, positive experience of having a Korean-American mother as a resource.

She's always come home and told me about things and we talk about ways that we can deal with things, and so we have this unspoken connection because of our common experiences. Actually, I probably do less than a lot of the white adoptive parents, as far as making her go to culture camp. I guess I don't have to do as much to keep her connected to her Korean-ness.

My daughter is very self-sufficient, and she'll make her own meals, and she will choose to make Korean food, or eat kimchi, just like she would pick up anything else. It's not like an occasion when she eats Korean food.

And, I have friends that are Korean, and friends that are non-Korean. When I'm with my Korean friends, I'm not with them just so she can be exposed to Korean culture. We get together just because they're my friends, and so that's a very different kind of thing, and that's what I really want adoptive parents to get . . . you don't get together with Koreans just because they have the added value that they're going to teach your child something. You do it because they're your friends.

My daughter's and my adoption experiences are similar in that we both have siblings who are our parents' biological children. I don't think that we necessarily talk about adoption any differently than I did with my mom, but I think that there's something different for her. When she talks about being adopted to other people, and tells people her story, she goes, "Yeah, my mom's adopted, my uncle's adopted, my cousins are adopted." I think for her to have that sort of

155

intergenerational experience normalizes it for her.

But, I don't think that I parent any differently than my parents did around the adoption issue. As far as differences between Brittany and my biological children, those that exist are, in my estimation, more a function of the fact that she was not part of our family for the first three years of her life. There are some definite formative issues that have arisen because of that, so it's not about whether she's adopted or not adopted. We do not have information about Brittany's birth family. Like me, she was abandoned. I know that a lot of adoption professionals cringe when you say that word, but I don't believe in political correctness. She was abandoned, abandoned in a train station.

And, it's interesting. Despite our openness about adoption, she has never expressed interest in finding her biological family. In fact, there's almost some anger there when I ask her. She'll say, "No, I'm not interested." And, I don't know if she's doing it to protect me, or if she's doing it because she really doesn't want to know or because there's anger there, and I have chosen to not address that with her, but just to accept her response. When she wants to talk about it more, I think she'll feel perfectly capable of doing that with me, but I get that at some level, there's a sense that she might feel like she'd be disloyal to me. But, she knows I would like to meet my birth family and I've told her why, so if she feels like she would be disloyal, I'm not sure where she would be getting that.

After she finished high school, Brittany made the decision that she was not ready for college, so she decided to go into the Air Force. The twins went in two different directions -- Rick also chose the Air Force and David went to the University of Missouri in Columbia, majoring in communications.

156

When I think about my siblings, Mark and I certainly were closest as far as chronological age, and I think we were always very close because of the common experience of being adopted. But I was always closest to my oldest brother, Bob, just based on personality. When you leave home, everybody goes their own direction and Bob's life is in a very different place than mine, so we really don't communicate very much. He retired from the Air Force and right now he's living out in Montana and working as a fly-fishing tour guide. I don't see him very often and he's not a communicator. It's sort of interesting because he married a woman who is half Chinese and I told him that he sees me in her. He also has a set of twins and another child as well.

My sister Kris and I were never particularly close when we were growing up. I don't know if we were competitive or what, but we just had a sibling relationship that was both antagonistic and playful. I always felt like she was the attractive one and I always felt insecure about that. We're both K's -- she wanted a sister whose name started with the same letter as hers. She was the blond, beautiful sister, a schoolteacher and married to her college sweetheart, a veterinarian. They have four children and live outside Minneapolis. She's not blond anymore, though. I wouldn't describe us as being close, but we get along,

Years ago a common friend of ours had made some comments about how beautiful Krissie is -- and I remember thinking, well, I must be really ugly then . . . obviously, I mean, you compare what is considered beautiful within a white context and from an Asian perspective. I just didn't like being short, and having a really round face and all that stuff.

I think that acceptance of my looks and confidence in my Korean-ness did not come for me until after I got divorced,

157

because I think within my marriage I felt somehow that my ex was making a concession or was overlooking the fact that I wasn't as beautiful as what *I thought* was beautiful . . . and so, it really wasn't until I divorced and started dating that I realized that people could really appreciate me for me.

When I think about my sister, she was always very good at school. She would get A's without putting a whole lot of effort into it, and I've always been a good student, but I've had to work really hard for it. One of the things I am, if anything, is tenacious. I'd have to work really hard for what I got and those things just seemed to come naturally to her, so there was that sense of tension. I guess I felt she was blessed, more so than I was.

Now I have my Ph.D., just like my dad, but I don't think that they expected it of me. In fact, if my dad were to choose one of us to go on and get a higher education, I don't think he would have chosen me. When we were living in England, I was 9 years old and I had this clarity about what I wanted to do with my life, which was a little scary. I knew that I wanted to get my Ph.D., knew that I wanted to adopt a child and knew that I wanted to work with people. I used say I wanted to be a psychiatrist, a psychologist or a hairdresser. I thought if my dad can get a Ph.D., I could do it. It was pragmatic, and although I've never processed this on a cognitive level, I guess part of it was a way to be accepted, to be valued for something that I could do. I've never had the direct message that I had to do that, from my parents certainly, but I think that my dad and mom will say how proud my dad is. When I was growing up, I got distinct messages from him that I wasn't the prettier one. Since I've accomplished my educational goals, I think it raised his esteem for me. My parents are living in northern Minnesota

158

now and I see them maybe twice a year.

Getting my Ph.D. means I'm able to be self-sufficient, especially as a single parent. I am in a good place now, in terms of myself and my career. For me, getting a Ph.D. was about being able to do what I want to do, which was research and teach, so it was a means to an end, as opposed to an end. I've done research about Korean adoption and I've actually collected some data about Chinese adoption too, so I'm looking at Asian adoption in general. I really think it's interesting to look at how the Korean and Chinese programs play out, and if Chinese adoptees will experience being adopted differently or in much the same way.

I've really sort of struggled with the adoption issue. Over the past few years I actually sort of came to terms with being a professional and a researcher and with not wanting to alienate the adoptive community . . . I want to be able to think critically about this. For me, it's like walking a tightrope because it's very easy to alienate the adoptive community if you're too critical, but then as a researcher, I have to ask certain questions.

I really think that I've sort of come to the place where I feel comfortable doing both, but from an integrity standpoint, one of the things that I will not do as a social worker is get involved in the actual practice of adoption. I will get involved in post-placement services, but not with adoption. If I did, how could I think critically about international adoption, raise the issue of neo-colonialism and ask difficult questions like: Is this really in the best interest of the child?

Kathleen Leilani Ja Sook Bergquist, 46
Associate Professor, School of Social Work
University of Nevada, Las Vegas

159

Frances

I remember when I had a family. When I was a small child, the oldest of three, we lived in a hut. So, I imagine my parents must have been farmers and peasants. I can see myself putting my baby brother on my back and looking out at the rice paddies while I was planting. These memories probably go back to when I was 6 years old.

Really early one day, perhaps when I was 7, my father took my belongings and left me on the doorstep of Star of the Sea Orphanage in Inchon, Korea. I don't think he explained anything to me. I just remember him taking me there and abandoning me.

I was so traumatized that I became very shy and very, very sheltered, and for six months or so, I spent a lot of time by myself -- even though I shared a room with about 20 children. I was

161

very, very quiet and I remember crying all the time. I was old enough to know that I had been left.

As it turned out, my father's action probably saved my life. I had tuberculosis, a disease my destitute family couldn't hope to cure. The Irish sisters who ran the orphanage restored my health, assigned me a birthday and pronounced me Park Sun Kum. The director, Sister Philomena, really was attached to me and thought I had tremendous potential as a human being. Getting me a private adoption became her cause and she prayed and pleaded with a lot of families. Even so, I ended up spending almost two years in the orphanage because it took that long before I tested negative for TB.

Eventually, I was adopted by a kind 66-year-old American electrician from San Bernardino, California and his wife. He'd been married before and had children who were already in their 40s when I came to the U.S. They had adopted a 2-year-old girl from Hong Kong a few years before and my father wanted to make sure my sister Mary Rose, who's a year older than I, had somebody to grow up with.

My parents took care of all my living and medical expenses while I was at the orphanage. They could have bowed out of the adoption because of my having TB, but they didn't. My father had literally picked my photo out of an annual report of the orphanage. He was flipping through the reports, saw this little face and said this was the little girl he wanted for his daughter. He said I had a look of sheer determination to succeed.

I still have that picture and from time to time I look at it to remind me of my very humble roots. Whenever I feel arrogance taking hold, I take it out. It's a very humbling experience to remind myself that if it weren't for the generosity of my parents, I might have ended up a concubine

162

or been pushed into child labor or out on the streets at age 12. Or even worse . . .

Actually, I believe that if I had stayed in Korea I could have been killed.

Even though I don't remember, I must have suffered lots of abuse in my biological family. When my parents took me to the doctor, he found scars on my body, old scars that shouldn't have been there. And, I know now, my scars weren't just physical. For five long years after my adoption, I had temper tantrums just about every day. Anything and everything would set me off -- for instance, my mother trying to discipline me. She would hit me and I couldn't take that.

I remember one time my mother was so frustrated when I was throwing my tantrums she threw a glass of water on me and said, "Just shut up. This household can no longer handle you throwing these outrageous temper tantrums. Shut up." I used to scream at the top of my voice, just scream, and somebody called the police. Finally the police realized that I was having a temper tantrum and that my parents were not beating me up. After awhile, the community just accepted the fact that I would have these outbursts. We had a trailer in the back of our house and when I was in the midst of a tantrum, my mother would put me in there and wait outside. I would exhaust myself and when I could calm down, I would come out.

I think the first year was probably the most difficult. Eventually all the discipline was left to my father who could calmly talk to me and explain what I was doing wrong. Very wisely my father took me to the local hospital. I saw someone and they followed me for years. Sometimes they came to the house and sometimes I went over to their office. If it weren't for that, I would not be who I am now. I think I

163

am more normal now, in spite of my childhood, because of these people who cared.

Unfortunately, I never developed a real emotional attachment to my mother. My father already had three children from his first marriage when he married my mother. Then they had two daughters and a son before adopting us when the others were already grown. So, my mother was involved in raising eight children. She always felt that my father, by adopting my sister and me, robbed her of her retirement. She was very, very close to her natural children and my sister and I have always been the outsiders. It wasn't good, but it's one of those things, like anything else, you accept.

My mother made sure my sister and I had all the provisions when growing up, but she was always distant and never really bonded with us. From the very beginning I was deathly afraid of her. I always kept a 5-foot perimeter between the two of us and never even sat near her. She was extremely fat, enormous really. She weighed over 300 pounds and I was terrified that she would fall over me and I'd be crushed to death.

One day my mother was upset that she felt I wasn't bonding with her physically. She told my father about it and he asked me. I told him the truth and my mother got quite upset. She had no idea her size would affect me this way. A week or two later she joined Weight Watchers. I don't know how many years it took but eventually she did lose weight. Later on my sisters and I -- four of us -- took pictures with all of us fitting into one of my mother's old dresses.

Right now my mother is quite elderly and has Alzheimer's. I go and visit her as much as I can, but she's not a real close part of my life. I think my sister feels the same way.

164

It's different with my father. He was always there for me, so I'd definitely say he's my favorite role model and hero. He died in 1979, but I still feel his presence and his spirit around me. My father and I always believed, and we talked about it several times, that our paths would continue to cross. When I'm having a tough time, I can always hear my father's voice. I think I would probably have had more blunders in my life, but he always managed to guide me spiritually. He's my guardian angel, even today.

My sister has a very difficult time going to my father's gravesite, but whenever I'm in southern California, it's the first thing that I always do. She thinks I have a major problem looking forward to visiting a grave, but I find tremendous tranquility when I go there. I drag my sister along, even though she just hates going. I always buy fresh-cut flowers and we always sing a favorite song together.

Perhaps surprisingly, my sister and I didn't have any idea when we were growing up that she was Chinese and I was Korean. Because many Asians stayed in the Los Angeles area, and we lived 60 miles northeast, we were always just about the only Asians in the whole school system. I remember only two others -- children from military families, who were half-Japanese and half-American. They stayed maybe a year.

My sister and I, and perhaps me in particular, thought we were German Catholics who happened to have slanted eyes. Slipping into that identity seemed logical to me. I knew that I was not Italian, not Hispanic and not African American. I identified with the German culture because we ate German food at home and my mother spoke German whenever she was upset. Her maiden name is Schmitt, and that's as German as it comes. We never ate any Asian foods

165

so to say that I was Asian would've seemed strange. Indeed, we had no Asian culture or people around us to reinforce that idea.

I really did not know anything about Chinese, Korean or Vietnamese people because I was never around them. I just figured I was different and the only explanation I ever got from my mother was that God had made my sister and me this way, that he had left us in the oven a little longer -- that's why we had darker skin.

Then, in the spring of fifth grade everything changed. My sister and I always walked the mile and a half to school together. A classmate of my sister's, a girl, started taunting her, shouting all sorts of names, like "Chinaman." This went on for about a month. She wouldn't stop and my sister was saying, "I don't understand why she's picking on me." I was a model student and would never pick a fight with anybody, but I guess I'd reached my threshold for frustration. Even though I was much smaller and looked about 8, instead of 12, I remember I just threw my books, climbed on top of the girl and beat the shit out of her. I yelled that she had no right to call my sister that name. I don't think I even knew what a "Chinaman" was! I just knew that it sounded very derogatory, very bad.

Many, many years after this incident I again came in contact with the girl who taunted us. She told me she'd never forget the experience. She was so shocked that somebody who was so much smaller actually beat the crap out of her. I told her that I don't even remember how I climbed onto her. It must have been my adrenaline just being so pumped up, because at that point I had simply reached my breaking point!

My parents were stunned that I had acted this way. I think that was the first time they realized that my sister and

166

I were starting to be aware that we were different, because other children pointed it out to us and made fun of us. It wasn't so much that my sister and I were saying we're different. Instead, it was brought out by the other children in our school.

When I think back I guess we must have been aware of it in elementary school when we looked at our class pictures and we stood out as the only ones with dark hair and slanted eyes. It was our yearly reminder. At some point all the pieces came together. We finally put all our feelings into words and said, "Pop, we're different."

I remember him bringing out the encyclopedia and showing us where Hong Kong was and then showing me where Korea was, and saying, "You came from here, a place called Inchon." And so, we were able to read from the encyclopedia about our roots. Finally, we saw pictures of people who looked like us, and then, I guess, that's when we realized maybe we're not German Catholics with slanted eyes anymore.

When this day came I think my parents were very, very open in letting us know as much as they knew about our backgrounds. I have my complete adoption papers, all the correspondence they sent to Korea finalizing the adoption, and all the checks they wrote supporting my activities and my medical bills. I think my father saved everything because he realized that one day we would want to know about our roots.

But, until we started asking, our parents didn't really do anything about helping us find out about our cultures. One of the difficulties they had was that there wasn't an abundance of Asians in our community. The only others were from a family who had also adopted five or six children, one from

167

my orphanage, a girl named Judy.

I knew her in Korea but I wasn't close to her because I didn't really have any social skills when I was there. She left about a year and a half before me. We were supposed to come on the same plane, but the TB forced me to stay behind.

She was the only connection that I had to the orphanage and our families would try to get together about three or four times a year. One year, she wasn't there, but everybody else was, and I asked, "Where's Judy, what happened to Judy?" Neither one of my parents wanted to say, but they finally told me she died. I don't know how. She was probably 16. When she passed away, I actually felt that I had nobody.

My only other link to my past was Sister Philomena from the orphanage. I communicated with her probably for about 20 years -- from the time I came to this country until she died. My mother really encouraged me to do that. I must have written in Korean at first and then gradually in English. We even saw each other a couple times. When she would come to the States my parents would arrange for us to meet.

Even though we're both adopted -- and both Asian -- my sister and I aren't close. She is very, very jealous of me because she felt that she wasn't given all the opportunities that I had. I find that incredible because she had, at least from my perspective, the same opportunities, but she wasn't motivated, wasn't disciplined, and just wasn't focused on what she wanted to do with her life. We had the same father and he spent a tremendous amount of time and energy on both of us, making sure that if there were a school project due, he would help us. He was very engaged and very involved with what was going on.

Still, my sister had no aspirations to go to college and,

168

actually, neither did I. The idea of going to college came to me by accident. I was engaged when I was in high school and I had insisted to my fiancé, who was three years older, that he be in college by the time I graduated. In my mind, that would give me a certain amount of security. But, when he wasn't moving in that direction by the time I was a junior, a light bulb went off and I thought, well, Frances, he's not going to do it, so you need to take care of yourself. I really started preparing for my SATs and buckled down in all my classes.

Finally my fiancé admitted he wasn't going to college so I broke off the engagement and decided to go myself. I come from a blue-collar family, so this was really uncharted territory. I'm still the only one in my whole family, including my many nieces and nephews, who has a college education. When I look back I realize that my determination to get an education came from my father, an electrician who didn't go beyond high school. I don't think he realized that he was so much ahead of his time. I remember him saying, "Frances, never depend on the man to take care of you because they will disappoint you. The only way that you're going to be ensured of having a future and to make something out of your life is to get an education yourself." My sister got the same message, but school was very frustrating for her, and she never wanted to excel because it was so much work.

When I think of some of the difficult encounters that I've had with my male counterparts, I know they've been amazed at the amount of internal strength that I have. This one person was incredibly difficult with me, creating so many hassles in my life. One night I took him out for a drink and I said, "Number one, you know nothing about me, but you're willing to harass me. I don't mind that; I know I'm

169

junior executive staff and you're essentially initiating me, putting me through the ritual, being in the big boys' club and everything.

"But," I said, "you need to understand one thing about me. I will out-survive you in this organization. You don't know who you're dealing with, and you don't know the sheer inner strength that I have because of my upbringing. You think you're going to break me with your childish games; they're nothing compared to what I had to go through." Then I talked with him about my childhood and he instantly stopped harassing and belittling me and making jokes, because he knew that my experience was beyond his imagination.

People couldn't believe that in one night this man had an attitude adjustment about me. But, I'd told him my mother tried to break me, to do things her way or no way. I'm one of these people that if you tell me what you want me to do, I'll do it. But, if you're only interested in the end result, please, let me decide how to do it. My mother said I was the most difficult child she ever raised.

The two of us had a tumultuous relationship during my teenage years. Mentally, I was the strongest of her children. She couldn't threaten me with a spanking. That meant nothing to me because spanking couldn't compare to what I'd received in the past. My mother said I had such sheer inner strength that she knew she could not break me down to the point where I would submit. Probably that's one reason why my teenage years were rebellious, not in drinking, smoking, getting pregnant, or going out late, but in trying to have an identity separate from my adopted family. I think sometimes that my mother wanted to protect me a great deal and didn't want me to grow up into an adult who was different from the values that they had in the Gipson-Schmitt family.

I was asking a lot of questions about Korea, about China. I was asking a lot of questions about those things that had very little relevance to the Gipson family, the Gipson home, my homework, or anything else in our family's life. It sort of distracted my parents because I was a very inquisitive child growing up and I always asked a tremendous number of questions. I used to ask my mother, in a curious, perplexed way, "Well, share with me, you know, what does being a Korean mean, what do these particular customs mean . . . the wild dances, the harvest festivals?" I'd be reading about it in a book, but I couldn't relate to it. I needed somebody, somebody who had more wisdom, to explain it to me.

Intellectually my mother could not appreciate that I was making my first attempts to learn about where I came from. I'd see some costumes people were wearing and I would drive my mother bananas because I would ask over and over, "Why are they doing those silly dances?" She didn't have a good way of communicating to me because it was totally foreign, and perhaps even frightening, that her child would be asking about a culture she knew nothing about.

I couldn't understand why my parents were reacting this way. I thought they knew everything in the world. I always had a lot of dialogue with them, much more than my sister did. I didn't realize that my mother didn't know about the festivals or the dances. Through all my formative years, every time I would ask a question, my parents had given me a response. After all, they had shared the details of our adoptions with us. But, this was the first time that I asked very specific questions about a culture and a language that neither one of them really knew much about. They were more clueless than I was.

I just wish that when I'd asked questions -- maybe after

171

watching a TV program about Korea, or reading an article in the encyclopedia -- they would have said, "We don't know, but why don't we go and ask somebody who would know?" Instead my mother would say, "I don't know and you have no reason to know, because it's not part of you." I would insist that it was supposed to be part of me, but she'd answer, "You're no longer in Korea, you're not Korean, you're American, you're being raised in a German-Catholic home. Why is it that you're so persistent in wanting information about something that you're never going to use? You have no reason to know."

I think that's when I became really rebellious, wanting to know more about something that I knew I was supposed to be part of. I just didn't know how to connect those lines or dots and because I really did not know anybody who was Korean, or even Asian, I could not go to anybody and say, "I need help."

Back in those days, we didn't have a computer to go on the Internet and search like we can today, and my father finally said, "You know, Frances, you need to stop doing that, you need to stop searching for something that isn't there. What you need to do is to focus on, you know, doing well on your SAT scores, and blah, blah, blah, blah, blah . . ." Because I loved and respected my father, I said okay. After about six months of driving them bananas, I quit trying and I put that in the back of my mind.

I try to visualize if I did go online and searched and found my birthparents, what is it that I would say to them? They don't know me as a human being and sometimes I feel that I just need to find them because they were that traumatizing to me. I know that one day, after having this one big tantrum episode, I told my father that I didn't know how

172

many more times I could do this and survive. How could I reintegrate the different parts of myself? I asked him if he thought I really had major psychological problems because of my childhood. I remember he compared my sister and me, saying that because she was only 2 when they got her she didn't experience any of the emotions that I was having. He used to say that he thanked the Lord for bringing me into this world and he always wanted to support me and wanted to be there. "You know," he said, "you know, pumpkin, (that was my nickname) sometimes, some journeys you have to do by yourself and this is one of them."

When I went to college, I started to rekindle my curiosity, especially in graduate school. I did see a couple of other Asian people, but they spoke very poor English, and I had difficulty understanding what they were saying. To befriend them, I would go to lunch with them, but I didn't know what they were saying because they had such heavy accents and also lots of difficulty understanding me. They were just incredibly smart and intelligent people to get into these programs, but they had difficulty articulating their thoughts. I tried to do several things with them socially but I just got terribly frustrated. So, I went through another identity crisis in my last year of graduate school.

One of my girlfriends was half-Korean and half-white and I used to go to their house and spent a little time with the family and the mother was able to satisfy some of my curiosity. I guess I'm one of these people that has an insatiable appetite for something, and if you feed me a little bit, I can say, yeah, I can live with that for a little while, and then it sort of springs up again. I think my identity crisis has followed that route of wanting information and getting a little bit of it, or, you know, sometimes just realizing that

173

there isn't any information. I think in my parents' situation, they just really did not have information to share with me and I just had to accept that, but it's been really an interesting road to travel -- to really try to identify my heritage and link my past with where I'm going in the future.

When it came to dating I really didn't encounter any prejudice because of my ethnicity. I truly believe that it has been just the opposite. I have had more than my share of men waiting to go out with me. Since junior high, I've never had a time when I didn't have a boyfriend or a significant other. I've never dated an Asian, an African American or a Hispanic American. I've always gone out with Caucasians.

I never considered myself to be a popular person. It's just that men have always been attracted to me. In fact, people who truly know me know that I'm actually really shy, that it takes a great deal from me to go out, to socially integrate. To this day my preference is to be by myself, and I have to force myself to engage and be with people. My girlfriends are really amazed that after all these years of knowing each other, I'm still very quiet, very shy.

Even today, even though I'm married, men will come to me and want to go out with me because they find me very sensuous and feminine. It's nice. I mean my husband specifically wanted to have an Asian wife. During the Vietnam period, he was around a lot of Asians, and he finds Asian women to be very soothing and very calming.

Although other people obviously identify me as Asian, I've spent 30 or more years focusing on a very busy career and personal life and being connected to other Asians was not a priority. It's only in the last few years that I've actually made a very conscientious and focused decision to really get to know my heritage, and to connect with people who are

Asian. It floors a lot of people when I say I made a strategic plan for my life. But, in my position as a health care executive, I've had to do strategic plans for many, many organizations. So, it comes naturally.

I remember on my 38th birthday I got up and made a strategic plan for myself. I was wearing my Victoria Secret nightgown. I had my flip chart, and I called work, told them I wasn't coming in and they were horrified. (Evidently they had a huge party planned.) I said, "I'm real, real grateful, but I need to spend time with myself because right now, I'm screwed up. I really am not focused on where is it that I want to go with my life. I don't know who I am and it's time that I spent a little bit of time with myself in trying to resolve some of the identity crises that I've been going through."

I really needed to say to myself that Frances Gipson is important, and I need to spend some time and energy devoted to that. As part of my strategic plan I decided that one of the things that I absolutely had to include in my life was to go back to my roots and my heritage. It was a very conscious decision on my part because I felt that I could not grow and evolve as a human being unless I knew who I was . . . to be able to accept the fact that I was Korean. Before that I really didn't accept it. I knew I was Korean. But, so what?

It's not that I was ashamed about being Korean. I've never been ashamed of anything that I've done or of who I am. It was just that I went through a major identity crisis at age 38, just as I had three times before -- when I came to this country, in high school and in my last year of graduate school.

Surprisingly, it happened for the last time when I was at the pinnacle of my profession as a health care executive. I had a very good marriage and I should have been on the top

175

of the world -- except I wasn't happy with what I was inside my heart. People who looked at me would never realize that I was having internal difficulties, trying to come to grips with being an Asian, and the fact that professionally, for the first time, I experienced discrimination because I was Asian.

That discrimination was a shock for me. I had a manager who told me that he could not work with me because I was Korean and he had lost some of his relatives during the Korean War. He said that because I was part of that, he could not like me, could not work with me, could not do anything with me. I couldn't believe that somebody was so angry with me because of a war that happened when I wasn't even a twinkle in somebody's eye. I was terribly sorry that he lost his uncle, and a brother in the war, but to take it out on me was so unfair. It was the first time that I was confronted with somebody telling me that I was Korean, and because of that, I had to be blamed for some of his loss.

I think that really sort of put things into perspective, making me realize that I knew so little about my heritage, so little about my background. This man's anger was absolutely so generalized, yet it was directed at me. I think that's when I was going through an identity crisis of saying to myself, "I'm Korean, but it's really pathetic that I know nothing about my roots, my heritage . . . I don't know other Koreans, or even other Asians."

I had been assimilated into the American culture so much that I didn't realize that I was different until somebody pointed out that I was very, very different. That's when I decided I really needed to decide who I was, to maybe trace some of my roots and to really start looking at other Asians, and discover what I may have in common with them.

One of my first steps was to take an introductory Korean

language course. Although I could read and write Korean as a child-immigrant, these skills were long buried and didn't even surface after I was exposed to my mother tongue. Through all of this, it often seems that I am in a dark room unable to find the light switch yet knowing absolutely that I am not blind.

After moving to Washington, D.C. in 1995, I deliberately set out to join various Asian/Korean organizations, hoping to find someone who could guide me into my past. In May 1997 I journeyed to Korea on a trip for adoptees sponsored by the Korea Society. I returned with a better understanding of how my country really couldn't take care of the many starving mouths of its children after the devastating Korean War. I know now that the love and tremendous courage of my country, and my natural parents, let me have a higher chance for a better life in a far-away country. The journey helped ease the bitterness of my abandonment.

My husband has urged me to go back to Korea again -- this time to Inchon, to the orphanage. He feels that it's really important for me to come to some closure because, he says, it's not healthy the way I have mentally blocked off faces and any identity of my birthparents. But, at the same time, he understands that this was a defense mechanism to cope with being abandoned and not having them in my life.

It's so crucial that I put some perspective into my childhood. I know there are ways of finding parents or relatives. I do have a picture of myself when I was found. But, that was so many years ago. I know in my heart that I will never see my birthparents or my birth brothers and sisters again. If I close my eyes I can actually visualize myself working out in the rice paddies, seeing the hut, seeing my little baby brother. But, I know nothing about them now.

Even so, after all this time I am coming back to my roots. I'm reminded that if it weren't for the gracious kindness of my adoptive parents, I would still be in the country, and I wonder what my life would be like. Would I be alive today? Doing what?

I can never forget, but what do I do with my past? Do I call it Memory 101 and put it on a shelf? I really don't know how to confront the essence of who I was.

It's not Frances Gipson. It's someone I was long ago . . . and I don't even remember my name.

Frances Gipson, 53
Health Care Consultant
Washington, D.C.

ABOUT THE EDITORS

Marilyn Lammert, MSW, ScD is a psychotherapist and healer in private practice and a former university professor. She has taught at Washington University, the University of Maryland, and the Catholic University of America. She and her husband, Paul Carlson, adopted their son, Adam, from Korea in 1983. Their daughter, Katie, was adopted domestically in late 1981. She and Adam are 7 months apart in age. In 1994 Dr. Lammert traveled to Korea with Adam and they began a search for his birth family. Two years later she went with Ellen Lee to Daegu, Korea where they met Adam's birthparents and one brother. In 1998 the entire family, together with Ms. Lee, traveled to Korea for a reunion with Adam's birthparents, two brothers, sister-in-law, niece and nephew. Adam's sister Katie has also met her birth families. Dr. Lammert lives in Bethesda, Maryland.

Ellen S. Lee, MSS, is a licensed clinical social worker. Korean-born, Ms. Lee came to the U.S. with her family at the age of 10. Ms. Lee's interest in Korean adoptees began when she met Marilyn Lammert and her adopted son, Adam, and became involved in their search for Adam's birth family in Korea. Though not adopted, Ms. Lee can relate to the adoptees' sense of disconnect from their birth country, loss of language and culture, and identity confusion. She lives in Chevy Chase, Maryland.

Mary Anne Hess is an award-winning freelance writer and editor. During her 35 years of professional experience, she has specialized in education and family issues. Her work has appeared in newspapers and education and parenting publications across the United States. She lives in Silver Spring, Maryland.